ENVISIONING
THE NEW ADAM

ENVISIONING THE NEW ADAM

Empathic Portraits of Men by American Women Writers

Edited and with Commentary by
Patricia Ellen Martin Daly

Foreword by Paula Hooper Mayhew

PRAEGER

Westport, Connecticut
London

The Library of Congress has cataloged the hardcover edition as follows:

Envisioning the new Adam : empathic portraits of men by American women
   writers / edited and with commentary by Patricia Ellen Martin Daly ;
   foreword by Paula Hooper Mayhew.
       p.   cm.—(Contributions in women's studies, ISSN 0147–104X ;
   no. 149)
   Includes bibliographical references (p.   ) and index.
   ISBN 0–313–29095–4 (alk. paper)
       1. Men—United States—Literary collections.   2. American
   literature—Women authors.   I. Daly, Patricia Ellen Martin.
   II. Series.
   PS509.M46E58   1995
   810..9′352041—dc20   94–37879

British Library Cataloguing in Publication Data is available.

A hardcover edition of *Envisioning the New Adam: Empathic Portraits
of Men by American Women Writers* is available from Greenwood Press,
an imprint of Greenwood Publishing Group, Inc. (Contributions in
Women's Studies, Number 149; ISBN 0–313–29095–4)

Library of Congress Catalog Card Number: 94–37879
ISBN: 0–275–95805–1

First published in 1995

Praeger Publishers, 88 Post Road West, Westport, CT 06881
An imprint of Greenwood Publishing Group, Inc.

Printed in the United States of America

The paper used in this book complies with the
Permanent Paper Standard issued by the National
Information Standards Organization (Z39.48–1984).

10 9 8 7 6 5 4 3 2 1

Copyright Acknowledgments

The editor and publisher gratefully acknowledge permission to reprint the following copyrighted material:

"Appraisal" from *Collected Poems of Sara Teasdale*. Copyright © 1926 by Macmillan Publishing Company, renewed 1954 by Mamie T. Wheless. Reprinted by permission of Macmillan Publishing Company.

"The Mutes" from *Denise Levertov: Poems 1960–1967*. Copyright © 1964 by Denise Levertov Goodman. Reprinted by permission of New Directions Publishing Corporation.

"By the North Gate" from *By the North Gate* by Joyce Carol Oates. Copyright © 1963 by Joyce Carol Oates. Reprinted by permission of John Hawkins & Associates, Inc.

"Poem for Granville Ivanhoe Jordan: November 4, 1890–December 21, 1974" from *Things that I Do in the Dark* by June Jordan. Copyright © 1977 by June Jordan. Reprinted by permission of June Jordan.

"My Father in the Navy: A Childhood Memory" from *Triple Crown* by Judith Ortiz Cofer. Copyright © 1987. Reprinted by permission of Bilingual Press/Editorial Bilingüe, Arizona State University, Tempe, AZ.

"The Gilded Six Bits" by Zora Neale Hurston. Reprinted by permission of Lucy Ann Hurston.

"A Tender Man" from *The Sea Birds Are Still Alive* by Toni Cade Bambara. Copyright © 1974, 1976, 1977 by Toni Cade Bambara. Reprinted by permission of Random House, Inc.

The story "A Tender Man" reprinted on pages 90–105 is from *The Sea Birds Are Still Alive* by Toni Cade Bambara, published in Great Britain by The Women's Press Ltd, 1984, 34 Great Sutton Street, London EC1V ODX, and is used by permission of The Women's Press Ltd.

"Parker's Back" from *Everything that Rises Must Converge* by Flannery O'Connor. Copyright © 1965 by Flannery O'Connor. Reprinted by permission of Farrar, Straus and Giroux, Inc. Copyright © 1956, 1958, 1960, 1961, 1962, 1964, 1965 by the Estate of Mary Flannery O'Connor. Reprinted by permission of Harold Matson Company, Inc.

"When He's At His Most Brawling" from *The Dog that Was Barking Yesterday* by Patricia Goedicke. Reprinted by permission of Patricia Goedicke.

"A Tree, A Rock, A Cloud" from *The Ballad of the Sad Cafe and Collected Short Stories* by Carson McCullers. Copyright © 1936, 1941, 1942, 1950, 1955 by Carson McCullers. Copyright © renewed 1979 by Floria V. Lasky. Reprinted by permission of Houghton Mifflin Co. and Floria V. Lasky. All rights reserved.

To Natalie

May your generation and your generation's children
enjoy more just and harmonious gardens.

CONTENTS

FOREWORD

> Only connect.
> —Epigraph to *Howard's End*, E.M. Forster

This anthology of stories and poems by women is unusual. It is shaped neither by a particular literary code nor by an overriding political ideology and chooses to reflect both the failure and the triumph of its shaping ideal: the achievement of personal empowerment through human connection.

Patricia Ellen Daly is her own brand of women's studies scholar, one of those women who has, from the first, linked her feminist intellectual interests with concerns for social and religious reform, the environment, pacifism, and animal rights. This collection of stories and poems speaks to her abiding belief in the shaping power of empathy in all human interaction with one another and the world we inhabit.

These works chosen by Dr. Daly reflect a variety of women and their points of view. Some of the selections demonstrate the destructive power of isolation and disconnectedness that is, and has been, the result of a history of gender socialization based on the differences between women and men. Other of the chosen works show the beneficent effects of affiliation, collaboration, and understanding between the sexes. In each, what has been called the "sex/gender system" is held up for close examination and, in the end, is put aside in favor of the amelioration of gender difference and the abandonment of the continued polarization of the sexes.

I hasten to add that advocating empathy between women and men has been seen as debilitating to women in some "second wave" literary feminist studies. Clearly, Dr. Daly has rejected this notion and has defined "empathy" as a positive force, clearly distinguished from "identification with the oppressor" or other of the more benign seductions of transferential identification with the powerful. Her vision, as demonstrated in the works that follow, urges peaceful

affiliation and the dissolution of armed gender camps. It is a good way to think
about men and women as we enter a new millennium.

Paula Hooper Mayhew
New York City, 1994

ACKNOWLEDGMENTS

This book has been a long time in gestation. Its birth has been midwifed by numerous people, whom I need to thank.

Paula Hooper Mayhew was particularly supportive of this book during its long and protracted gestation, when so many other necessary tasks and responsibilities took me away from nurturing it. In recent years, as I have been able to devote more time to it, Steve Smith of Claremont McKenna College and my loving colleagues and supportive administrators at Neumann College have encouraged me in many ways, intellectually, emotionally, and practically.

I am particularly grateful to the Faculty Development Grant Fund of Neumann College and to the Chace and Western Quarter Education Funds of Philadelphia Yearly Meeting for their help in meeting the high costs of permissions to reprint literary works these days and to Ellen Kuhl for her assistance in locating the owners of some of the rights to these works.

I am also grateful to Professors Michael Heller of Roanoke College, Langdon Elsbree of Claremont McKenna College, and William Lynch of Neumann College for their careful readings of and reactions to an earlier draft of my commentary. I wish to also thank Professors Susan Day Dean and Anne Dalke of Bryn Mawr College for serving as sounding boards to some of my ideas concerning the congruences between Quaker and feminist ideals and Professor Leon Forrest of Northwestern University for his help in identifying works of African-American women writers on this theme.

Many people have generously helped in the production of this manuscript. In particular, I wish to thank Mary Ann Tini, Karen Babiak, and Juliana Smith. Without their devoted, meticulous typing, this book would never have come to be. I am especially grateful to Juliana Smith, who patiently, scrupulously produced the final, camera-ready copy. I also owe a debt of gratitude to Mary Hopkins for help with the index and to the librarians at Neumann College, especially Craig Conrad, who helped me locate much of this research.

Neumann's Director of Computing, Tony Patti, has also given generously of his time and advice to help me produce this book.

Also, I am very grateful to Marilyn Brownstein, George Butler, and Peter Coveney and Elisabetta Linton, my editors at Greenwood Press, who have steadfastly supported and assisted this project.

Finally, I wish to thank my significant other, Gene Hillman, all the members of my family who have encouraged me unflaggingly, and in particular my daughter who has insisted that she and other equally ardent feminists of her generation critically want and need this book.

To all of you, I thank you for making this birth possible.

Patricia Ellen Martin Daly
Newark, Delaware, 1995

ENVISIONING
THE NEW ADAM

INTRODUCTION

Some years ago, while reading yet another explanation of "The Eternal Female" by a man, I began to wonder: Have women ever tried to define men throughout history? Curious, I began leafing through books by women that might have something to say about men. I soon found that the answer was yes. Women, especially American women, had plenty to say about men. But in contrast to male pronouncements on women, women's statements on men (prior to the last few decades) have tended to be quieter, more musing, more speculative—and quite penetrating. Conveyed for the most part through the prisms of literature and art, rather than the window grilles of philosophy and psychology, these female perceptions of the male as a corpus of work have been largely overlooked. Particularly neglected in literary anthologies and criticism are American women writers' perceptions over the past century of men's virtues, dilemmas, and paths to happiness. Equally neglected are the contributions of American women writers to a central myth of American culture, the Adamic myth of America as the New World Garden of Eden. Such neglect has prompted this collection.

Do American women writers value and sympathize with anything in men as traditionally gendered? As I began this study not only in the early years of the second wave of American feminism, but also as the brunt, personally, of much awful treatment by men, I thought the answer to that question was simple: very little. I was surprised. Operating within the theoretical framework of feminist theory and readers' response literary criticism, I closely examined over 275 stories, poems, and novels by women featuring men. I found that there was a significant line of male protagonists with whom their female creators seemed to empathize.

Perhaps they were created as imaginary models of what men would need to do to deserve a woman's admiration and/or compassion. Perhaps they were patterned after some real-life father, brother, lover, or friend whose virtues the patterner wished to hold up for emulation and whose dilemmas she wished to plumb more fully. Some—particularly those who become trapped in their dilemmas—may have been created by some gifted women driven to exasperation by the good men in their lives seemingly hell bent on sabotaging their potential as men. I do not know.

I do know that many other readers whom I have encountered besides myself find themselves responding with sympathy to the male protagonists portrayed in this collection. While many of these male and female readers are highly educated in the conventions of literary interpretation, some are not. Most, however, seem to manifest, like myself, many of the traits of "constructed knowing" described by Mary Field Belenky and her colleagues in *Women's Ways of Knowing* (131–52). As such, their responses to these stories and poems are highly informed by empathy as defined by Nel Noddings—i.e., empathy as "reception," rather than "projection." Describing herself as an empathetic knower, Noddings says: "I receive the other into myself, and I see and feel with the other" (30). Seeing and feeling "with the other" have led many readers of the works collected here to perceive the male protagonists they portray as meriting sympathy. Is this the only way of interpreting these stories and poems? By no means. As great works of art, they lend themselves to a variety of interpretations that deepen our wisdom about the human experience.

The process in readers of seeing and feeling with literary characters is generally guided by narrative conventions, as well as by the conventions of literary interpretation. Thus, when a reader encounters a character who is described approvingly or in beautiful, lyrical language or with gentle humor, that reader is more inclined to feel friendly toward that character. Similarly, characters whose painful feelings we are told a great deal about and whose sufferings are openly commiserated with and/or related in great detail generally evoke our sympathy. In addition, we often find ourselves caring more about characters who are esteemed and/or anguished over by other characters we admire. Likewise, when we encounter characters who are associated with lyrically described settings, as M'sieur Michel in "After the Winter," we often find ourselves feeling more kindly about them and their dilemmas. The same is true of characters who are linked with figures who historically command respect, as O.E. Parker is with Christ in "Parker's Back." These are but some of the textual clues that helped prompt sympathetic responses in me as well as in the colleagues and the many students with whom I have read these works. In the commentary that precedes each section in this anthology, I have identified some of these intertextual clues with regard to each literary work.

In the case of short stories, what also most shapes our response is plot, and most particularly the way the protagonist resolves his or her dilemma and changes. How we perceive the protagonist's central predicament and resolution of that predicament is guided further by our value systems and our understanding of human psychology. If the protagonist we care about struggles with problems we recognize other people to have and resolves them in ways that correspond to our values, we tend to like them even more. As I show in the rest of this introduction, the quandaries confronting the characters in these stories have been identified by gender studies scholars such as Carol Gilligan, James Doyle, Sam Keen, Victor Seidler, and Lillian Rubin as typical of American man as traditionally gendered. And as I further show, the new Adams here who struggle into states of greater happiness do so in accordance with feminist value systems identified by such scholars as Gilligan, Rubin and Josephine Donovan. Therefore, it is probably not surprising that many women and non-sexist men have responded equally sympathetically to these men as have I, a feminist student of gender studies.

Who am I as a reader? I am Caucasian—or as my late African-American friend Mary Ann Williams liked to say, "non-melanin" as opposed to "melanin." I am largely middle class with working-class roots and a single parent's experience of the extreme feminization of poverty during the past thirteen years. In addition to intellectual studies, I write feminist fairy tales and conduct research on Ruth Suckow, a twentieth century "lost" woman writer. I have also actively participated in women's policy making for the National Center for Policy Alternatives as well as multicultural community development. And while it is true, as Paula Hooper Mayhew suggests in her foreword, that I am driven by no particular literary code or political ideology, I do operate within certain traditions and have affinities with certain feminist positions within what Annette Kolodny calls the "happy pluralism" of feminist approaches to literary theory (19).

Fundamentally, I am a feminist in the Quaker tradition. That is my primary theoretical framework. I currently teach at a Franciscan college that began as a women's college and embodies governing values that have many commonalities with Quaker and feminist values. Although it has not yet been extensively documented by scholars, Quaker feminism has richly contributed to the development of feminist thought and practice, particularly in North America. As Margaret Hope Bacon details in her book *Mothers of Feminism: The Story of Quaker Women in America*, (1986) four of the five women who planned the Seneca Falls convention of 1848 were Quaker. So were Susan B. Anthony and Alice Paul. Although Paul (and Abby Kelly Foster) later resigned from the Religious Society of Friends, she remained Quaker-identified all of her life (Bacon, *Mothers* 201). According to Bacon, Jane Addams, first chair of the Women's Peace party, "was the daughter of self-styled Hicksite John Addams," who although "never a member of a Quaker meeting . . . maintained close ties with Quakers throughout her life" (*Mothers* 147). Jane Addams mentored Quaker Mildred Scott Olmstead, the driving force behind the development of the Women's International League for Peace and Freedom (Bacon, *One Woman's Passion* 155) and Olmsted shared some of her wisdom with me when we both attended the same Friends Meeting from 1988 to 1990.

Quaker feminism is a very strong vein of American feminism. The preponderance of Quaker women in the leadership of the early American feminist movement was not a coincidence. Since its founding by George Fox, Margaret Fell, and other seventeenth-century British men and women, the Religious Society of Friends has believed that there is "that of God" in everyone—male and female as well as people of all races and skin colors. Putting that belief into practice (which has not occurred as quickly or as fully as it should have) resulted in Quakers tending to view women as equal to men and striving to effect social and political changes that would make that equality a reality. Thus, from the seventeenth century on, for instance, Quaker women were revered as church leaders, preachers, and ministers. In the United States, from the seventeenth century on, such female preachers were often financially enabled by their meetings to leave their often large broods of children and household duties to the care of their husbands while they "traveled in the ministry" (Bacon, *Mothers* 24–41). Shortly after the establishment of the Pennsylvania colony by Quakers, Philadelphia Yearly Meetings set up schools in Philadelphia for blacks and whites of both sexes (Bacon, *Mothers* 59), initiating an early tradition of Quaker coeducation in the United States. Throughout the nineteenth century, Quakers helped pioneer the education of women at the post secondary level by founding or helping to found Oberlin, Antioch, Bryn Mawr, Earlham, and Swarthmore Colleges and numerous other smaller Quaker colleges throughout the country (Bacon, *Mothers* 98–100).

As both Howard Brinton and Bacon point out, because so many of the educated, assertive women in nineteenth-century North America had been educated in Quaker-run or Quaker-influenced schools and/or through the exercise of leadership in the Society of Friends, nineteenth-century feminists were greatly influenced by Quaker values (Bacon, *Mothers* 2; Brinton, *Friends* 150).

What are these Quaker values that have exercised so great an influence upon my vision of the texts in this anthology and upon the American women's movement? In *Mothers of Feminism*, Margaret Hope Bacon describes them as

> the use of nonviolence in protecting the early conventions against angry mobs, the insistence on including women of all races and walks of life in meetings, the tradition of working for consensus rather than making decisions hierarchically, the ties between the women's movement and the peace movement, the tendency toward a broad rather than a narrow focus on issues. (2)

In addition, while Quaker feminists have not hesitated to angrily confront men about the subjugation of women, they have not generally felt a need to cut themselves off from men as potential partners in the work of transforming society's gender-related oppression. Says Bacon: "Beginning with George Fox, many male Quakers have shared the struggle for equality. Quaker feminists today insist that this struggle is the duty of both men and women" (*Mothers* 4). In addition, Quaker men have always been expected to reject many of the most oppressive aspects of the male gender role prescribed by the patriarchy.

Explains Bacon:

Out of the same spiritual roots as the testimony on the equality of women and men in the Society of Friends came a set of values traditionally regarded as "feminine." The practice of love, humility, empathy, peacemaking and philanthropy has not been set aside for women only, but has been shared by men and women equally. Friends have believed that these are in fact Christian values to which all owe allegiance. . . . To wed . . . assertiveness and love as Jesus did, is the dream today of many Quaker men and women. (4)

In recent years, as Donovan describes in *Feminist Theory: The Intellectual Traditions of American Feminism*, American feminist thought has grown more and more consistently to emphasize a distinctive cluster of values. Many of those values, which Donovan describes in her chapters "The New Feminist Moral Vision" and "The Eighties and Beyond," are values that Quakers also share. Among these are a reverence for Nature and very different epistemological approaches than those embraced by the prevailing patriarchal modes of knowledge construction.

Quakers regard the experience of truth as something that emerges from, among other things, those sources that, according to Donovan, feminists also value: an orientation of attentive "waiting" and a cherishing of individual empirical experience and diverse personal perspectives (172–183). Current theories regarding women's epistemology, as characterized by Donovan, emphasize many orientations prized by Quakers. Says Donovan:

A substantial body of evidence has been produced that suggests that women's judgements are based on a fundamental respect for the contingent order, for the environmental context, for the concrete, everyday world. Women more than men appear to be willing to adopt a passive mode of accepting the diversity of environmental "voices" and the validity of their realities. Women appear less willing to wrench that context apart or to impose upon it alien abstractions or to use implements that subdue it intellectually or physically. Such an epistemology provides the basis for an ethic that is non-imperialistic, that is life-affirming and that reverences the concrete details of life. (173)

Describing the process for seeking truth in a Quaker meeting for business, a process that originated in the seventeenth century, Brinton sounds many similar emphases:

The business before the meeting, presented by the clerk, a committee or an individual, is "spoken to" by those who have opinions or judgement regarding it. . . . Dogmatic persons who speak with an air of finality, or assume the tone of a debater determined to win, may be a serious hindrance. Eloquence which appeals to emotion is out of place. Those who come to the meeting not so much to discover truth as to win acceptance of their opinions may find that their views carry little weight. Opinions should always be expressed humbly and tentatively in the realization that no one person sees the whole truth and the whole meeting can see more of the truth than can any part of it. (*Friends* 106–108)

A major difference between Quaker and feminist epistemologies, however, is that the Quaker search for truth, especially in a business meeting or a meeting for worship, should be motivated primarily by a "waiting on the Lord," who is regarded as the source of each individual's perception of the truth, as well as of the underlying, greater, but yet unperceived truth, in which all differences can potentially be reconciled.

Because I am a Quaker feminist, I tend to value empathy as well as anger, including empathy for men. In addition, because I feel a great need to remain open to the truth from all sources, I am not inclined to particularly adopt any one theoretical framework within literary criticism and feminist theory. I am, however, most drawn to the theories of cultural feminism as described by Donovan (*Feminist Thought* 31–63)—which is probably not surprising, since many of the mothers of these theories whom Donovan cites, such as Addams and Sara Grimke, were Quaker-identified. While I have concerns about extreme female separatism, I like the blend of male-female arrangements within Quakerism, which Bacon says nurtured so many of the first-wave feminists: ergo, separate Quaker women's and men's business meetings as well as business meetings governed by men and women together (*Mothers* 42–54). While I also worry about the claim that women can "purify politics" through the approaches of cultural feminism, I believe that the moral vision identified by Donovan as feminist needs to prevail over patriarchal moral codes, described well, I think, by Sam Keen as espousing the following tenets:

- Western culture has been dominated by patriarchy—rule by the men, of the men, and for the men.
- Patriarchy is rooted in hierarchy, obsession with power, control, and government by violence.
- Warfare, rape and biological destruction of "Mother" nature are rooted in patriarchal habits of thought and modes of social organization.
- Misogyny and gynophobia—a devaluation of all things considered feminine—form the subtext of Western his-story. (196)

Within feminist literary tradition, I feel some sympathy for what Sara Mills terms the "critical approach" of "authentic realism." A proponent, like many Quakers and feminist activists, of "plain language," I resonate to the suggestions Mills says some groups within "authentic realism" are making: "Any feminist work should be written in such a way that all women will be able to understand it and put it into practice. Complex theoretical terms should not be used, since this type of language and approach to knowledge is typically patriarchal; in the way in which it excludes women, it has historically been one of the elements in their oppression" (53).

Finally, I agree with Elaine Showalter's assertion in *Speaking of Gender* that it is time for some feminist literary scholars to investigate the "ways that reading and writing, by men as well as by women, is marked by gender" (2) as well as to undertake "serious inquiries into masculine modes of creativity, interpretation and representation" (7) as a "step further toward post-patriarchy" (11). In addition, I agree with Showalter that this is a step "worth trying to take together" (11). Therefore, I have presented papers on the subject of this anthology at the annual Men's Studies Conference sponsored by the pro-feminist National Organization of Men Against Sexism (NOMAS) and at the 1991 Friends Association for Higher Education (FAHE) Conference.

My presentation at FAHE was followed by what the authors of *Women's Ways of Knowing* would probably term a "connected teaching" experience. This is an experience that Belenky and her colleagues feel enables participants to "construct truth not through "consensus" whose original meaning, Norman Holland reminds us was, "feeling or sensing together," implying not agreement necessarily, but a crossing of the barrier between ego and ego bridging private and shared experience" (223). In this consensual exploration at FAHE, men and women met in separate groups to discuss the issues raised by my paper, with the men facilitated by Dr. Steve Smith, a philosophy professor and teacher of men's studies who has also presented at NOMAS, and the women led by the late Dr. Alice Wiser, a founder of *Ovum Pacis*, the Women's International Peace University. Then Steve and I conducted a brief "structured dialogue" on some of the questions explored by the men's and women's groups. As a result of this process, participants reported greater insights into the characters in these works—and into themselves.

Who are the male protagonists presented here, what are their problems, how do they solve them, and what is the significance of their solutions? In some of these stories, the good men resolve their dilemmas in ways that lead to happiness; in others, men of promise throw away their chances for happiness through foolish decisions. Put together, therefore, these works begin to reveal not only what many American women writers seem to value in men, but also what they see as some possible paths to happiness for their brothers. In addition, these stories and poems seem to constitute a much overlooked contribution by women to the "new Adam" myth, which many scholars feel has helped shape North American culture. Much fuller and more insightful portrayals of such men and such paths are available in novels like *Shadow of a Man* by May Sarton and *Mama Day* by Gloria Naylor, but, unfortunately, the requirements of the anthology genre do not permit their presentation and analysis here.

Many of the sympathetic portrayals of men I found in my study were by women who had created some fairly disagreeable male protagonists in other works—Flannery O'Connor, for instance, and Joyce Carol Oates. So the appearance of a relatively worthy man in the midst of their corpora really caught my attention. Were these then portraits from the same authors of more agreeable men?

Equally striking was the general absence of any romanticism, idealization, or sentimentalization of agreeable men by women writers. There are no "Angels in the House" and certainly no Natty Bumpos here. There are no pedestals under the feet of any of the men in this collection. Instead, their creators tend to be rather matter-of-fact, down to earth, and clear-eyed about them, calmly observant of their faults as well as their virtues and possibilities. This attitude is probably best captured in the poem by Sara Teasdale, which I have included: "Never think she loves him wholly," says Teasdale; "Never believe her love is blind/All his faults are locked securely/In a closet of her mind."

The men portrayed here by American women are depicted with generally unblinking realism—literally complete with all their failings. So none of the men presented in this anthology is an unqualified hero. Do not expect to be swept off your feet by their nobility and majesty. At best, they are struggling—trying, often desperately, to understand themselves and the world around them and, where successful, to learn what they need to learn and to change, usually laboriously, for the better. Not a one of them is unimpeachable, and many of them, like Parker in "Parker's Back" and Carson McCullers's unnamed protagonist, are mean and unpleasant in the beginning of their stories, only learning painfully and slowly how to be human beings whom women can esteem more. The overriding fable in the second half of this collection, in fact, seems to be that of men who are initially benighted seekers, but who variously yearn for, grope toward and sometimes stumble into states of greater wisdom and goodness.

What positive qualities do these qualified heroes exhibit—either from the beginning or as a result of their arduous self-transformations? Many of these qualities—sensitivity, gentleness, kindness, vulnerability, and warmth, for instance—are familiar to us proponents of the "New Man" of the "New Age," especially noteworthy here because we see how clearly they were admired also by women of previous eras. In addition, there are, in such characters as Zora Neale Hurston's Joe Banks, a host of qualities more commonly associated with the "Pre–New Age Man": he who was more lauded for being firm, open, frank, vigorous, robust, straightforward, resolute, brave, self-reliant, hard-working, honest to the point of bluntness, steadfast, loyal, honorable, and of rock-hard integrity. Intertwined with these are the "sweetness" of Banks, the emerging tenderness of Toni Cade Bambara's Cliff Hemphill, the earnestness of McCullers's protagonist, the wistfulness of Willa Cather's Paul, the simplicity of O'Connor's Parker—and above all the passionate and often innocent yearning for something holy of so many of them. It is that yearning for something to revere, inchoate and inarticulate as it so often is, that seems to constitute their most saving grace in the eyes of their female creators.

All of the men in these literary excerpts yearn deeply for something special outside of themselves that will enlarge and enrich, if not transform, their lives. As I show in greater detail in later commentary, most of the men in these selections seem initially isolated, disconnected, self-centered, and bent on controlling the significant people and events in their lives. In addition, when we first meet them, they generally cannot define what they are longing for, often are unaware that they so yearn, and are almost always, at the outset, unable to identify and communicate these feelings along with other feelings. Very few seem happy or aware of what will bring them happiness.

The saddest figures among these male characters are those whose yearning is misplaced or never gets them anywhere. Sarah Orne Jewett's Tom Wilson longs unsuccessfully to be free of restrictive gender roles and to enjoy happiness with his unconventional wife. Cather's Paul craves a life of beauty, a life scorned by his Philistine father and friends, and settles for a few delusionary days, rather than a more fruitful pursuit of it. Oates's Revere also experiences futile and inchoate yearnings for something beautiful and/or holy in his life.

Many of these men, however, are drawn by their yearnings toward a world radiant with such things as natural beauty; a comforting, warm home life; ardent feelings, especially love; and, most markedly, relationships and connectedness—in short, toward the things especially valued by women according to such feminist scholars as Donovan. Often living, like Parker and McCullers's protagonists, initially isolated, lonely, unfulfilling, and rather selfish lives, these men suddenly find themselves more and more dissatisfied and restless, until they give in and respond to their unclear yearnings. In so responding, they are often overtaken by strange, unsettling new sensations and feelings. They sometimes start doing things they cannot explain—as when O.E. Parker suddenly, inexplicably marries Sarah Ruth the day after he swears he will never do so. More often than not, they find themselves groping through this new, uncertain territory. Frequently, their journeys are sharply clarified as the result of a crisis or a confrontation with a perceptive, outspoken woman. After a period of struggle, during which they relinquish at least some of their insistence on control, they emerge with a new orientation to life. Generally speaking, this new orientation involves a growing ability to let go of their too exclusive reliance on such things as stoicism, cynicism, detachment, self-containment, unyielding self-determination, and a constrained, cramping concentration on their work life. In their place, they learn—above all—to love. In addition, they are often more able to seek relatedness with other living creatures, to "go with the flow" more, to care about others even if it means risking being hurt, and to think things through more for themselves, particularly ethical matters.

In recent years, many gender scholars have identified the dilemmas resolved by these transformations with the male gender role, as that role has been traditionally determined by the patriarchy. In his textbook *The Male Experience*, Doyle, for instance, brings together a very impressive array of evidence from research over the past twenty-five years to create a portrait of the gendered male, particularly in postindustrial society. Many of the features of this portrait correlate with qualities found in these portraits by nineteenth- and twentieth- century female authors. Postindustrial men, Doyle shows, were "expected to become the sole provider for their family's material needs" and thus became overinvolved with their work lives (1973). Such overidentification, among other causes, has given rise to an overinvestment by men like Parker in their work, rather than in their relationships with family and others (Doyle 244). In *Fire in the Belly*, Keen also outlines how success in work has become identified with establishing self-worth for a man (51–67).

Western male socialization has also required men to suppress "emotions that leave a person open and vulnerable to others . . . emotions like love, pain, tenderness, sadness, sorrow, compassion, joy" (Doyle 157–58). Such socialized repression, as well as homophobia and social ills, has forbidden men to exhibit caring behaviors toward other men (Doyle 161). Such gendering exacts a heavy price, as Doyle shows: "Most men go out of their way to keep people, men and women alike, at an emotional arm's distance" and as a result suffer from much isolation and loneliness (162–63). Such is only too clearly the case with men like Cather's Paul and Oates's Revere.

Drawing on the theories of Melanie Klein, Nancy Chodorow, Dorothy Dinnerstein, and others, Rubin attributes similar qualities to the Western male as currently gendered. "Most men," she says in *Intimate Strangers: Men and Women Together*, "are not very good at interpersonal negotiations that are laden with emotional content because their inner relational life was left relatively impover-ished by the need to repress their early primary identification with mother" (63). To defend himself psychologically against the pain caused by such repression, a man "builds a set of defenses" that include "barriers that rigidly separate self from other, that circumscribe not only his relationships with others but his connection to his inner emotional life as well" (Rubin 56). Consequently, men become more invested in their work lives than in their intimate relationships because, says Rubin: "Work is rational and cognitive, love is emotional and experiential. Work is mastery, achievement, competition, separateness; love is sensory, feeling, sharing union" (164).

Finally, in his searching critique of structuralist theorizing entitled *Rediscovering Masculinity: Reason, Language and Sexuality*, Seidler sounds many of the same themes. Says Seidler:

> It is important to recognize that at a level of personal experience and engagement in relationship, the invisibility to themselves that results from men's power and propensity to impersonalize and universalize their own experience tempts them into constantly talking for others, while presenting themselves as the neutral voices of reason. This constitutes a limit to men's experience, for it precludes them from grasping the particularity of their experience and its social and historical sources. This could be a source of learning and the base of the development of a different relation to self and individuality, which would involve drawing on the insights of a psychoanalytic tradition which has too often been dismissed as essentialist in contemporary and particularly post-structuralist social theory, and which can help us to understand that masculinity is an essentially negative identity learnt through defining itself against emotionality and connectedness. (7)

Like the men in many of these stories, post-Kantian men, according to Seidler, have been estranged from self, personal experience, "emotionality," and "connectedness"—because of Kant's "account of the human subject as split irrevocably between reason and desire" (2) and the subsequent excessive "identification of masculinity with a particular conception of reason" (14). In the post-Enlightenment institutionalization of relationships "between reason, science, progress and masculinity," Seidler maintains, "The experiences of women, children and animals have been closely identified as lacking reason, and being closer to nature" (14). Such institutionalization and subsequent identification have led to the notion that men must dominate Nature and women (25) and try to control their emotional and somatic lives by ignoring them as "anti-rational" (49). Seidler feels that in *Madness and Civilization* Foucault gives a historical account of the patriarchal expectation that men subordinate "a femininity which is identified with nature, with emotions and feelings, with desire" (80).

The New Adams in the stories collected here struggle to overcome this maddening estrangement from self, Nature, women, and emotional and somatic states by turning their backs on patriarchy's command to dominate and control such entities.

If the American female's New Adam reflects many of the more harmful characteristics of the post-Enlightenment male gender role, he embraces qualities and orientations that many gender scholars see as highly valued by women. Chief among these orientations, according to Donovan is a "consciousness that is relational, contextual, integrative and life affirming" (89). Such a consciousness, says Donovan, is highly valued by such theorists as Nancy Harstock, Nancy Chodorow, Rosemary Radford Reuther, Sara Ruddick, Carol Gilligan, and others (89–90). Donovan sees the conclusions of the above theorists as correlating with those expressed by Harstock in *Money, Sex and Power*: "Harstock's 'feminist standpoint' is derived from women's 'experience of continuity and relation with others, with the natural world, of mind with body,' an experience that provides an ontological basis for . . . a social synthesis that needs not operate through the denial of the body, the attack on nature, or the death struggle between self and other" (90).

Donovan sees a number of feminist theorists as perceiving this relational consciousness as leading to a "fundamental respect for the contingent order, for the environmental context, for the concrete, everyday world" (173). In Kathryn Allen Rabuzzi's theories, Donovan perceives the identification of a female sensibility that "involves an adaptation to contingency where one flows with the waves" (174). Ruddick's "maternal thinking," according to Donovan, "involves a reverential respect for an immediate, daily, other reality to which one accedes an independent validity, on which one does not attempt to impose total control" (175).

This is the state that such New Adams as McCullers' protagonist seem to emerge into: an orientation of greater connectedness with reverence for, and non-controlling "go with the flow" attitude toward all of inner and outer reality.

In addition, such New Adams seem to evolve into the greater "ethic of care" and experience themselves within the "web of life," which women value, according to Gilligan and others.

In her groundbreaking *In a Different Voice* Gilligan envisions this particularly female orientation as a consciousness of self within "a network of connection, a web of relationships, that is sustained by a process of connection" (32). In contrast to the male "emphasis on separation rather than connection," females tend to consider "the relationship as primary" and to view morality as "concerned with the activity of care" (Gilligan 19). According to Gilligan, this "ideal of care is . . . an activity of relationship, is seeing and responding to need, taking care of the world by sustaining the web of connection so that no one is left alone" (62). Such an ethic leads women to value interdependence over a rigid independence (167).

Interdependence with all of creation is the state McCullers's protagonist has struggled into—and the state he suggests that all men strive for.

According to Donovan, most contemporary feminists are headed in the direction of championing interdependence among all living things; i.e., "towards a more comprehensive view that recognizes the interrelationships among all living beings, and the right of all to exist" (208). To convey this view, Donovan quotes a 1990 ecofeminist manifesto entitled "A Declaration of Interdependence": "Humankind has not woven the web of life; we are but one thread within it. Whatever we do to the web, we do to ourselves. Whatever befalls the earth befalls also the family of the earth" (208).

According to the second account of creation in the Bible, the last time the "family of the earth" experienced harmonious interdependence within the web of life was when God "planted a garden in Eden" and created "every animal of the field and every bird of the air" as possible partners for the Adam (or generic Human) God had made to "till" and "keep" this garden (Genesis 2:1–25). In her groundbreaking study *The Land Before Her: Fantasy and Experience of the American Frontiers, 1630 – 1860*, Annette Kolodny has extensively demonstrated that the image of America as a garden to be created and tilled to support human interdependence was elevated to the status of myth by a number of early to mid-nineteenth century American women writers. The twentieth and late nineteenth century stories and poems in this collection constitute, I believe, another invitation to men to shake off their patriarchal gendering and to join women in the female approach to restoring this garden. While they do not preclude a viable male approach to restoration of the natural world, the works here also constitute, I suspect, but the beginnings of a narrative, contextual blueprint for the approach to that restoration by women.

What is also unique about this collection, I believe, is what literature always has to offer over the social sciences: the revelation that some women discerned, and at least intuitively understood, male dilemmas and transformations long before the social scientists did—and understood them sufficiently to be able to capture them with a degree of individualizing detail that generally must escape the rigorously "objective" methodologies of the social scientist. In addition, these richly detailed, empathic, and compassionate portraits invite us to do something else the social sciences cannot always get us to do very well. By bringing to life men who elicit our good will and sympathy, men so lovingly drawn that we find ourselves identifying with them in all their joys, sorrows, and quandaries, and by focusing as much on solutions to male dilemmas as on the dilemmas themselves, gifted women writers lead us to respond to the male plight with our hearts, and with hope. And as both these writers and gender studies scholars are pointing out, men who approach life's challenges with more hope, love, and openness are more likely to experience value and meaning in their lives, and perhaps even be happier.

As I have noted, many of the male characters who undergo positive transformations in these stories evolve into happier, more caring human beings more in harmony with themselves, women, other men, and, often, all of creation and God—or at least they demonstrate a much greater openness to this particular transformation. Very often these men are portrayed as journeying to, or opting to stay in, rural settings where their lives seem to be more nourished and vitalized by a loving engagement with Nature. Conversely, many of the men who fail to undergo positive transformations in response to the crises in their lives are depicted at the end of their stories in rural settings, but devitalized and still disconnected, even from the nourishments of their natural settings. The message, therefore, seems to be this: Undergo this kind of transformation, and you can return to a state that resembles, at least partially, the Garden of Eden—a state in which both men and women are able to live in greater harmony within themselves, with each other, and with all of creation. As such, these works by American women writers strike me as a distinctly female contribution to what scholars like Judith Fryer call the "dominant myth of American culture," the "myth of America as the New World Garden of Eden" (ix).

The "myth of America as the New World Garden of Eden" has been perceived by numerous scholars and researchers as a myth that has strongly shaped American culture. R.W.B. Lewis, David Noble, Leo Marx, and Annette Kolodny are but a few of the people who have identified this myth as one that has fed the ways North Americans view themselves and thus has helped to chart the course of North American history.

In R.W.B. Lewis's view, the Adamic myth "saw life and history as just beginning. It described the world as starting up again under fresh initiative, in a divinely granted second chance for the human race, after the first chance had been so disastrously fumbled in the darkening Old World" (5). In this myth, the American Adam, according to Lewis was "an individual emancipated from history . . . untouched and undefiled by the usual inheritances of family and race; an individual standing alone, self-reliant and self propelling, ready to confront whatever awaited him with the aid of his own unique and inherent resources" (5). Lewis sees James Fenimore Cooper's "Deerslayer" as the penultimate Adamic hero, a "self-reliant young man . . . whose characteristic pose . . . was the solitary stance in the presence of Nature and God" (91). Later writers, particularly Nathaniel Hawthorne, Herman Melville, Henry James, and William Faulkner, portrayed more complex Adams, according to Lewis. In Hawthorne's *Marble Faun*, says Lewis, the Adamic hero experiences a "fall" that can be claimed as fortunate because of the growth in perception and moral intelligence granted the hero as a result of it (127). In Melville's *Billy Budd*, Lewis mentions, "the American hero as Adam became the hero as Christ" (130).

In *The Eternal Adam and the New World Garden*, Noble concurs with much of Lewis's conception of the Adamic myth, emphasizing the importance of close ties to Nature for the New World Adam. Says Noble, "This exceptional hero was to gain the strength for breaking his personal and social bonds by achieving organic union with nature; he would tap the vast power of the earth mother," (4) and, thus, the "great and magnificent expanse of virgin land" (4) in the American West was "a limitless national reservoir of spiritual strength" (5).

Both Lewis and Noble see nineteenth- and twentieth-century male writers as criticizing this Adamic myth. Noble believes that Cooper, Hawthorne, and Melville "deny that America can become a New World Eden . . . they refuse to believe in the perfectibility of man" (6). Fryer sees American writers from 1840 to 1900 as struggling primarily with "the urge toward perfection" and maintains that to such writers who "in novel after novel recreated the Garden, either in newborn pristine and somewhat sterile innocence or in its Old World state of decadent experience, the myth of America as New World Garden was so central to the American imagination that it permeated all levels of culture, consciously and unconsciously" (xi).

According to Annette Kolodny our understanding of the Adamic myth has been shaped largely by our preoccupation with male writers who have viewed the American land as a "virginal paradise to be opened" and conquered as an immensely nurturing mother (*The Land Before Her* 3-4). Because of the incestuous conflicts such configurations posed, many early American male writers, Kolodny suggests, cast the American New Adam as the "isolated woodland son, enjoying a presexual—but nonetheless eroticized—intimacy within the embrace of the American forest" (5). In the 19th century, Kolodny demonstrates, "in their promotional writings, as in their domestic novels set in the west, women writers stripped the American Adam of his hunting shirt and moccasins, fetching him out of the forest and into the town" (9). In their works women like Lydia Sigourney and Maria Susanna Cummins created American Adams who rejected the "plundering" of the wilderness for profit and instead joined forces with women in creating peaceful settlements among the "parklike and flowered expanses alternating with stands of trees" of the American prairies. Instead of mythic portraits of the male "individual standing alone, self-reliant, and self-propelling" (Lewis 5) in "the presence of Nature and God" (91), the image which arises from the women's works Kolodny analyzes is "the enticing image of a flowered prairie paradise, generously supporting an extended human family, at the center of which stood a reunited Adam and Eve" (*The Land Before Her* 9).

To analyze how this Adamic myth plays out in American literature, Lewis and Noble examine only male writers. Fryer, who focuses on the fact that "only Adam resided" in this New World Garden (ix) gives us an analysis of women in the works of nineteenth-century male writers, with the exception of her explication of Kate Chopin's *The Awakening*. Kolodny is the only scholar who seems to have examined, in a highly public forum, the uniquely female contribution of a number of American women writers to the Adamic myth. However, her analysis focuses primarily on some early and mid-nineteenth century female authors. We need more scholarly examination of the contribution of a wide array of American women writers to the Adamic myth. It is time for that examination. It is time also, I suggest, to revise the Adamic myth in the light of feminist Biblical scholarship, of scholarship on the Quaker influences on this myth and of the contributions of Native Americans, African-Americans, and other writers of color to the envisioning of America as a potential second Eden.

Feminist Biblical scholars like Elaine Paegels have helped us to see that the misogynist readings of Genesis, which have prevailed since Augustine, were an aberration, a deviance from the original belief of the first four centuries of Christians that the "primary message of Genesis 1 to 3 was that of freedom: freedom in its many forms, including free will, freedom from demonic powers, freedom from social and sexual obligations, freedom from tyrannical government and from fate, and self mastery as the source of such freedom" (xxv). In Colonial America, New England Puritans most embraced the dark view of the Garden of Eden story, which Augustine shaped, the view that "Adam's sin not only caused our mortality but cost us our moral freedom, irreversibly corrupted our experience of sexuality (which Augustine tended to identify with original sin) and made us incapable of genuine political freedom" (xxvi).

And, unfortunately, Puritan visions are what have most shaped our understand-ing of American culture. Although, for instance, Robert Spiller in *The Roots of National Culture* acknowledges the influence of other early American traditions such as the Quaker tradition, he maintains that Puritanism was "probably the most enduring of many elements in seventeenth and eighteenth century thought in America" (4). However, just as American feminism has strong Quaker roots, and, therefore, feminist visions of ideal humans are congruent with Quaker values, so does one whole thrust of American culture have Quaker roots. Inattention to compelling Quaker influences on American culture may have a great deal to do with the alignment of the Puritan ethic, according to E. Digby Baltzell, with patriarchal, hierarchal, legalistic, rationalistic modes of operating, while the Quaker ethic was more associated with egalitarianism, "sex equality," and an emphasis on the Gospel's message of "love and feeling" (94). In his groundbreaking study *The Quaker Influence in American Literature*, Howard Hintz notes: "From Colonial times to the present century, the list of American authors who were Quakers or the immediate descendants of Quakers is an imposing one. The prominence and the importance of the Quaker strain in American letters is a subject which up to the present time has not been fully recognized or adequately treated" (5).

Part of this greatly unresearched "Quaker strain" in American literature is the Quaker conception of the Garden of Eden story. Fell alludes to this Quaker view of the Creation myth in her 1666 pamphlet "Women's Speaking Justified, Proved and Allowed of by the Scriptures. . . ." Forcefully arguing for the right of Quaker women to preach in public, Fell anticipates here many of the positions of contemporary feminist Biblical scholars regarding the respect women commanded in both the Old and the New Testaments as prophets and preachers. Fell also points out eloquently that God made no distinction between men and women "in the first creation" (Wallace 65) and the same is truer in the "new creation" (Wallace 65) issued in by Christ (whom Fell and other Quakers routinely referred to as the Second Adam (Wallace 60). Fell and other Quaker founders saw the Second Adam as a model for all, male and female alike, and believed themselves to be calling Christianity back to the early, communal, caring, egalitarian life of men and women pictured in the *Acts of the Apostles*.

According to Brinton, Fox divided history into three eras: "that before Adam's Fall when man existed in the image of God, that after the Fall, when man was ruled by outward laws and rituals, and, thirdly, that marked by the coming of Christ, the second Adam" (32). During the second period, the period of the old covenant, people were warlike, legalistic, and given to male domination, among other things. But the period of the new covenant, initiated by Christ, was supposed to change all that; the problem was that as of Fox's time, many Christians had not yet moved on to embrace the new covenant, but were still stuck in the old covenant. Those who truly espoused the new covenant were able to become joyful, good, uncorrupted human beings. To explain Fox's philosophy, Brinton says (using the non-inclusive language that was common in 1973): "Man fell from 'Christ the substance' the timeless reality that existed before Creation, through the first Adam. But by coming into unity with Christ, the second Adam, man could rise to a higher state than that of the first Adam. Before his fall, the first Adam was guiltless because he was innocent; but the second Adam was higher than he" (35).

The belief that people could "rise" up into the Edenic state of the second Adam is what supports the Quaker optimism and belief in the "perfectibility" of humans that Baltzell sees as contrasting so sharply with Puritan pessimism about fallen man (94). It is also one of the beliefs that powerfully informed the Holy Experiment, the founding of Pennsylvania by William Penn, and the shaping of American democracy in Philadelphia.

Penn, Fox and Fell were friends and greatly influenced each other. First written as a preface to Fox's *Journal* in 1694, Penn's essay "The Rise and Progress of a People Called Quakers" echoed Fox's vision of the three eras of history: that of the first and second Adams with the period of the Old Testament intervening (Tolles and Alderfer 7–43). When Quakers in England were persecuted for their efforts to call all Christians to espouse the "New Covenant," Penn looked to found a colony in the New World where Quakers would be free to put their beliefs into practice. According to William Wistar Comfort, he was persuaded in part to choose Pennsylvania as the site of his new colony by Fox and other Quaker missionaries who had travelled to the New World to preach (21). The Holy Experiment, according to Frederick B. Tolles and E. Gordon Alderfer, allowed Penn and other Quakers to demonstrate to the world how a Christian society could be erected on the radical foundation of the Sermon on the Mount, a realization of "a New Testament society of love and peace and freedom" (100). Pointing out that Penn's 1682 "Preface to the First Frame of Government in Pennsylvania" makes deliberate references to the first and second Adams, Tolles and Alderfer say that the Quaker settlers whom Penn envisioned "might be expected to live lives of primitive innocence like that of Adam before the fall"; they also suggest that Penn viewed Pennsylvania as a re-creation of the "Garden of Eden" (107–8).

There is some evidence that Penn himself viewed the early years of the Holy Experiment as Edenic, as a time when all people, settlers and Native Americans alike, lived in peace and harmony surrounding the "green countrie towne" of Philadelphia, which he described in these Edenic terms: "The soil is good; air serene and sweet from the cedar, pine and sassafras, with wild myrtle of great fragrance. . . . Fish in abundance, especially shad and rock oysters are monstrous for bigness. In the woods are diverse fruits wild, and flowers that for colour, largeness and beauty excel" (Tolles and Alderfer 39). Penn may very well have viewed his Holy Experiment as one likely to finally issue the third major epoch of history, the period of the second Adam finally espousing the new covenant.

Just as the feminist values the men in these stories struggle with are congruent, in large measure, with Quaker values, I suspect that these female visions of the American New Adam are congruent with the Quaker, and not the Puritan, interpretation of the Garden of Eden myth. Some of this congruence has been suggested recently by Jane Atteridge Rose in her study of Rebecca Harding Davis. Commenting on the ending of Davis's 1861 "Life in the Iron Mills," in which a serene, loving Quaker woman appears in the prison cell of the oppressed ironworker and suicide, Hugh Wolfe, and takes his devastated widow away to her peaceful, rural Quaker community, Rose says:

> A recurring figure in Davis' fiction, this Quaker woman embodies the author's vision of social reform arising out of moral reform. . . . The Quaker woman enacts the mystery of love and the power of individuals to make a difference. Though a stranger to the Wolfes and their sordid world of poverty, crime and death, she comforts Deborah. To Deborah, who has hungered for love, she offers the hope of a new life after prison in her community of Friends. Though Hugh has been lost to the system, Deborah can still be saved. . . . The last scene . . . asserts a reformative plan implicit in much of Davis' fiction, in which society is restructured on feminine principles: sentimental theology, spiritual integrity and agragarian familial communities. (21)

Finally, except for Noble's criticism of James Baldwin as "hysterically affirming" a useless, "antique faith" in the Adamic myth (225–26), little scholarship seems to have been done on the contributions of African-American writers to the envisioning of America as a potential New World Eden—or on the participation of other writers of color in the shaping and/or examination of this myth. Study of the participation of such writers in this envisioning needs to be done with an erudite understanding of history and of non-Euro-American cultures—after all, Native Americans were here cherishing the "New World Garden" within the framework of their religious beliefs long before Puritans or Quakers or other religious groups arrived to "re-create" the Garden. And African-Americans were by and large dragged here against their wills; their slavery in American cotton fields and elsewhere hardly demonstrated an effort to recreate Eden. Nevertheless, the heroic transcendence of their barbarous treatment by many African-Americans such as Martin Luther King, Jr., through a Christianity faithful to the Gospel and through other means has enabled, I suggest, a very special and critically needed contribution to the Adamic myth.

"I call this approach a New Covenant," proclaimed Bill Clinton, describing his vision of a better America in his "A New Covenant" speech to the Democratic National Convention in July 1992 (Clinton and Gore 226). Notions of the "New Covenant" and of America as the New World Garden of Eden are still alive and well in our culture. It is time to revisit them in the light of contemporary Biblical scholarship, of feminist scholarship, and of scholarship in the contributions of Quakers and of people of color to the Adamic myth and to American culture. Most especially, it is time to revisit them in the light of what American women writers have had to say about the merits and promise of the male-gendered American New Adam.

This framework of values and theoretical sympathies out of which I operate accounts, in part, I think for this reader's selection of the particular stories in this anthology. My final choices were also governed by other factors. I wanted, for instance, to include stories and poems illustrating this theme from many traditions other than the Anglo-American.

My experiences as the aunt and great-aunt of African-American females and my years working for African-American and Hispanic communities and organizations have taught me that I fall short of interpreting well the cultural expression of women of color: however, I felt *Envisioning the New Adam* called for contributions from American women writers from as many different backgrounds as possible, however inadequately I might interpret those works in my commentary. Many of the stories and poems by women of color that portray men sympathetically, however, were written during the past twenty-five years and cost a great deal to reprint in an anthology. Thus, I was forced to leave out a number of literary works by women of color. I do not know what the solution is to this complicated situation, but I do know that the economics of securing permissions, particularly for recent works, are making it very difficult for scholars to assemble academically oriented anthologies, and that is unfortunate.

Because this collection initiates new directions in scholarship, and because it was prepared under serious economic constraints, it lacks, I am sure, many works that ought to be presented here. I apologize for that and invite others to point out appropriate works and to join me in the postpatriarchal work of studying empathic portraits of men by women writers and of revisiting the American Adamic myth. Much is to be gained by this study.

WORKS CITED

Bacon, Margaret Hope. *Mothers of Feminism: The Story of Quaker Women in America.* New York: Harper & Row, 1986.

――――. *One Woman's Passion for Peace and Freedom: The Life of Mildred Scott Olmstead.* Syracuse, N.Y.: Syracuse University Press, 1993.

Baltzell, E. Digby. *Puritan Boston and Quaker Philadelphia.* New York: The Free Press, 1979.

Belenky, Mary Field et al. *Women's Ways of Knowing.* New York: Basic Books, 1986.

Brinton, Howard. *Friends for 300 Years.* Philadelphia, Pa.: Pendle Hill Publications, 1965.

――――. *The Religious Philosophy of Quakerism.* Wallingford, Pa.: Pendle Hill Publications, 1973.

Burt, Struthers. *Philadelphia: Holy Experiment.* New York: Doubleday, Doran & Co., Inc., 1945.

Clinton, Bill, and Al Gore. *Putting People First: How We Can All Change America.* New York: Times Books, 1992.

Comfort, William Wistar. *The Quakers: A Brief Account of Their Influence on Pennsylvania,* ed. Frederick Tolles, rev. Edwin B. Bronner. University Park, Pa.: The Pennsylvania Historical Association, 1986.

Donovan, Josephine. *Feminist Theory: The Intellectual Traditions of American Feminism.* 2nd ed. New York: Frederick Ungar, 1992.

Doyle, James. *The Male Experience.* 2nd ed. Dubuque, Iowa: William C. Brown, 1989.

Fryer, Judith. *The Faces of Eve: Women in the Nineteenth-Century American Novel.* New York: Oxford University Press, 1976.

Gilligan, Carol. *In a Different Voice: Psychological Theory and Women's Development.* Cambridge, Mass.: Harvard University Press, 1982.

Hintz, Howard. *The Quaker Influence in American Literature.* Westport, Conn.: Greenwood Press, 1970.

Keen, Sam. *Fire in the Belly: On Being a Man.* New York: Bantam Books, 1991.

Kolodny, Annette. "Dancing Through the Minefield: Some Observations on the Theory, Practice and Politics of a Feminist Literary Criticism." *Feminist Studies* 6 (1980): 1–25.

――――. *The Land Before Her: Fantasy and Experience of the American Frontiers, 1630 – 1860.* Chapel Hill, N.C.: The University of North Carolina Press, 1984.

Lewis, R.W.B. *The American Adam: Innocence, Tragedy and Tradition in the Nineteenth Century.* Chicago, Ill.: University of Chicago Press, 1955.

Mills, Sara, et al. *Feminist Readings/Feminists Reading.* Charlottesville, Va.: University Press of Virginia, 1989.

Noble, David W. *The Eternal Adam and the New World Garden*. New York: George Braziller, 1968.

Noddings, Nel. *Caring*. Berkeley, Calif.: University of California Press, 1984.

Pagels, Elaine. *Adam, Eve and the Serpent*. New York: Random House, 1988.

Rose, Jane Atteridge. *Rebecca Harding Davis*. New York: Twane Publishers, 1993.

Rubin, Lillian B. *Intimate Strangers: Men and Women Together*. San Bernardino, Calif.: Borge Press, 1990.

Seidler, Victor J. *Rediscovering Masculinity: Reason, Language, and Sexuality*. London and New York: Routledge, 1989.

Showalter, Elaine, ed. *Speaking of Gender*. New York: Routledge, 1989.

Spiller, Robert E. *The Roots of National Culture*. New York: Macmillan, 1933.

Tolles, Frederick B., and E. Gordon Alderfer, eds. *The Witness of William Penn*. New York: Macmillan, 1957.

Wallace, Terry S., ed. *A Sincere and Constant Love: An Introduction to the Work of Margaret Fell*. Richmond, Ind.: Friends United Press, 1992.

PART ONE

POTENTIAL, BUT UNTRANSFORMED NEW ADAMS

Of all the men portrayed sympathetically by women, the saddest are those whose struggle for happiness does not bear fruit. The male characters in this section yearn to enlarge their hearts and spirits, groping for someone or something outside themselves to give their lives meaning and joy—but either latch on to the wrong object or seem to lack the strength to fully pursue their search. They possess the potential to become New Adams in the New World Garden of Eden, but fail to realize that potential.

Denise Levertov seems to capture the tenor of these men's lives in her poem, "The Mutes." "Those groans men use," she says,

> passing a woman on the street
> . . . . . .
> to tell her she is female
> . . . . . .
> are they a sort of tune,
> an ugly enough song, sung
> by a bird with a slit tongue
>
> but meant for music?
>
> Or are they the muffled roaring
> of deaf mutes trapped in a building that is
> slowly filling with smoke?
> Perhaps both.
> . . . . . .
> . . . her understanding
>
> keeps on translating:
>
> 'Life after life after life goes by

without poetry,
without seemliness,
without love. '

The saddest of all these "birds with slit tongues," to my mind, is Willa
Cather's adolescent Paul. Sensitive, idealistic, drawn to the arts, Paul leads an
isolated, loveless life in a very ugly section of Pittsburgh, surrounded by people
who seem to have no idea of what makes him tick. Alone with his emotionally
distant, blue-collar, Philistine father since the death of his mother, Paul pursues
his dream of a life of beauty in secret. "In Paul's world," Cather tells us, "the
natural nearly always wore the guise of ugliness," so "a certain element of
artificiality seemed to him necessary in beauty." He finds his Eden in the theater
and concert hall, "secret temples" that constitute for Paul "his bit of blue-and-
white Mediterranean shore bathed in perpetual sunshine"—the shore the
exploitative capitalists bask on while Paul's father and men like him toil wearily
to keep the greedy capitalists rich.

When his father makes him quit his job as an usher, Paul stupidly steals some
money in order to live out his dreams for a few days in a luxurious New York
hotel—in a room rather metaphorically filling with smoke. Trapped when he runs
out of money, friendless, bereft of the life of "poetry" he craves, Paul flings
himself in front of a moving train. Perhaps his young, sensitive soul has been too
damaged by the harshness around him, perhaps the capitalistic system has
crippled him and/or lured him into false Edens or perhaps he simply lacks the
strength to pursue his yearnings in a more successful way. We do not know, but
a boy so clearly "meant for music" who yearns as passionately as Paul does for
a life of beauty and peace, situated in a less patriarchal, capitalistic society and
more able to reach out to others and to find beauty in less expensive sources,
would be more capable of "slit-tongue healing" and Adamic transformation.

Equally "meant for music," but ultimately untransformed, is Tom Wilson of
Sarah Orne Jewett's 1884 story "Tom's Husband." Unlike Paul, Tom seems to
have a better shot at somewhat Edenic happiness, but he loses it because he is
unable to sufficiently defy the stifling conventions of the patriarchy. During his
engagement to his wife Mary, we are told in the beginning of the story, Tom
experienced bliss, as did Mary. They longed "to have each other to themselves,
apart from the world, but it seemed that they never felt so keenly that they were
still units in modern society. Since Adam and Eve were in Paradise, before the
devil joined them, nobody has had a chance to imitate that unlucky couple." Part
of Tom's premarital happiness stems from his great affection for "qualities" in
his wife that would have displeased some other men, namely her independence,
self-reliance, "executive ability," and "uncommon business talent."

The "devil" joins Tom and Mary in the form of the old mill Tom's father has
left, which his sister feels represents a neglected investment—and in the form of
society's unwillingness to approve of the Wilsons' role reversal when the
physically lame and visually handicapped, unambitious Tom allows his enter-

prising wife to take over the mill while he takes charge of their domestic life. "For a good while Tom enjoyed life," content with this arrangement, Jewett tells us, "and went on his quiet way serenely." Then taking care of this house in this peaceful rural setting becomes a burden to him—despite the fact that he had done it quite cheerfully when he lived in it as a bachelor. As his wife becomes more successful and preoccupied with operating the mill, Tom does not turn to other people to sustain his emotional well-being and becomes more withdrawn, isolated and discontent. He stops pursuing his interests and loses contact with former friends; metaphorically speaking, he feels his "house" to be filling with smoke and himself to be trapped. He concludes that he has "merged his life in his wife's," Jewett tells us, and "he lost interest in things outside the house and grounds . . . he had a suspicion that he was a failure." Recognizing that this is "almost exactly the experience of most women," Tom both resents having to experience a female "lot" and feels "a new, strange sympathy" for his mother. A compliment from his stepmother, however, on his excellent housekeeping prompts Tom to order his wife to leave the mill and spend the winter in Europe with him—thus banishing both of them from the more paradisiacal life they might have experienced if Tom had been better able to resist the suffocating restrictions placed on men and women by the patriarchy.

In Joyce Carol Oates story "By the North Gate," the farm that constitutes the world of her untransformed New Adam is literally and figuratively "burning up" and suffocating its sole inhabitant in the process. Unlike Cather's Paul, sixty-eight-year-old Revere had apparently once enjoyed some meaningful human relationships—with his wife, his three children, and a young school teacher who taught him to read when Revere was thirty. But his wife has died, his sons have left, his daughter has married, the school teacher has been driven away by a violent student, and Revere has chosen to "await death" on his ever more decrepit farm, refusing his daughter's invitation to live with her. Increasingly weak, subject to fainting spells and memory losses, Revere is preyed upon by some young bullies who first slit his dog's ears and set his field on fire, and then kill his dog, cruelly inviting him to notice it. Trembling with horror and fury, Revere shouts after the murderers, "You come back! Come back here! All my life I done battle against it: that life don't mean nothin! That it don't make sense!" The painfulness of his situation is eased by his warm memories of arguing with the schoolteacher about life, and Oates ends the story with this sentence: "All the strange failures of his life, all its picking torment, even this final vexatious waiting for death—all shrank before his memory of that time, the way his childhood nightmares had shrunk back, vanquished, before the clear empty sunshine of the day."

Admirable though Revere may be for his warm memories, his fierce insistence that life has meaning and even, perhaps, for his stubborn desire to remain independent on his farm, we are left with a number of questions: For example, if reading and discussing philosophical questions with the schoolteacher gave him glimpses of Eden, why doesn't he connect with someone now with whom he can experience these joys? If he loved his children when they were young, why doesn't he reach out to them now? If he loves his farm so much, why doesn't he bring other people to it to help him "cultivate his garden"? Isn't there anyone who can help stop this cruel victimization of him by the local bullies? Despite the fact that he is still struggling for meaning and that he once experienced at least some glimmers of "poetry, seemliness and love," which he clearly yearned for and enjoyed, Revere has allowed himself to slip back into a life of disconnection and bleakness. Should the bullies continue to escalate their violence toward him, he may soon find himself literally trapped in "a building that is slowly filling with smoke."

In all these works by Levertov, Cather, Jewett, and Oates, the males seem to be relatively decent people with potential—potential to become wiser, more loving people who are more able to develop their unborn gifts and more able to throw off the oppressive restrictions of the Old World and seize the opportunity to create new opportunities for happiness for all in the New World. To develop their potential, however, these thwarted New Adams would need to respond to the deep yearnings within them and reach outside themselves to connect warmly with other sources of wisdom, love, and joy in fruitful ways. Their failures to respond successfully to these inner yearnings plunge them into weakness, ill health, or death. In picturing their sad devitalization so coolly and attentively, their female creators seem to be gently holding up a mirror in which all of us, and particularly men perhaps, can see the tragic results produced by a male socialization that overemphasizes self-reliance, control, separateness, a task orientation, and inattention to the inner self. Making such a mirror available to us in such a way strikes me as an act of great compassion.

APPRAISAL

Sara Teasdale

Never think she loves him wholly,
Never believe her love is blind,
All his faults are locked securely
In a closet of her mind;
All his indecisions folded
Like old flags that time has faded,
Limp and streaked with rain,
And his cautiousness like garments
Frayed and thin, with many a strain—
Let them be, oh let them be,
There is treasure to outweigh them,
His proud will that sharply stirred,
Climbs as surely as the tide,
Senses strained too taut to sleep,
Gentleness to beast and bird,
Humor flickering hushed and wide
As the moon on moving water,
And a tenderness too deep
To be gathered in a word.

THE MUTES

Denise Levertov

Those groans men use
passing a woman on the street
or on the steps of the subway

to tell her she is female
and their flesh knows it

are they a sort of tune,
an ugly enough song, sung
by a bird with a slit tongue

but meant for music?

Or are they the muffled roaring
of deaf-mutes trapped in a building that is
slowly filling with smoke?

Perhaps both.

Such men most often
look as if groan were all they could do,
yet a woman, in spite of herself,

knows it's a tribute:
if she were lacking all grace
they'd pass her in silence:

so it's not only to say she's
a warm hole. It's a word

in grief-language, nothing to do with
primitive, not an ur-language;
language stricken, sickened, cast down

in decrepitude. She wants to
throw the tribute away, dis-
gusted, and can't,

it goes on buzzing in her ear,
it changes the pace of her walk,
the torn posters in echoing corridors

spell it out, it
quakes and gnashes as the train comes in.
Her pulse sullenly

had picked up speed,
but the cars slow down and
jar to a stop while her understanding

keeps on translating:
' Life after life after life goes by

without poetry,
without seemliness,
without love.'

PAUL'S CASE

Willa Cather

It was Paul's afternoon to appear before the faculty of the Pittsburgh High School to account for his various misdemeanors. He had been suspended a week ago, and his father had called at the Principal's office and confessed his perplexity about his son. Paul entered the faculty room suave and smiling. His clothes were a trifle outgrown, and the tan velvet on the collar of his open overcoat was frayed and worn; but for all that there was something of the dandy about him, and he wore an opal pin in his neatly knotted black four-in-hand, and a red carnation in his buttonhole. This latter adornment the faculty somehow felt was not properly significant of the contrite spirit befitting a boy under the ban of suspension.

Paul was tall for his age and very thin, with high, cramped shoulders and a narrow chest. His eyes were remarkable for a certain hysterical brilliancy, and he continually used them in a conscious, theatrical sort of way, peculiarly offensive in a boy. The pupils were abnormally large, as though he were addicted to belladonna, but there was a glassy glitter about them which that drug does not produce.

When questioned by the Principal as to why he was there, Paul stated, politely enough, that he wanted to come back to school. This was a lie, but Paul was quite accustomed to lying; found it, indeed, indispensable for overcoming friction. His teachers were asked to state their respective charges against him, which they did with such a rancor and aggrievedness as evinced that this was not a usual case. Disorder and impertinence were among the offences named, yet each of his instructors felt that it was scarcely possible to put into words the real cause of the trouble, which lay in a sort of hysterically defiant manner of the boy's; in the contempt which they all knew he felt for them, and which he seemingly made not the least effort to conceal. Once, when he had been making a synopsis of a paragraph at the blackboard, his English teacher had stepped to his side and attempted to guide his hand. Paul had started back with a shudder and thrust his hands violently behind him. The astonished woman could scarcely have been more hurt and embarrassed had he struck at her. The insult was so involuntary and definitely personal as to be unforgettable. In one way and another, he had made all his teachers, men and women alike, conscious of the same feeling of physical aversion. In one class he habitually sat with his hand shading his eyes; in another he always looked out of the window during the recitation; in another he made a running commentary on the lecture, with humorous intent.

His teachers felt this afternoon that his whole attitude was symbolized by his shrug and his flippantly red carnation flower, and they fell upon him without mercy, his English teacher leading the pack. He stood through it smiling, his pale lips parted over his white teeth. (His lips were continually twitching, and he had a habit of raising his eyebrows that was contemptuous and irritating to the last degree.)   Older boys than Paul had broken down and shed tears under that ordeal, but his set smile did not once desert him, and his only sign of discomfort was the nervous trembling of the fingers that toyed with the buttons of his overcoat, and an occasional jerking of the other hand which held his hat. Paul was always smiling, always glancing about him, seeming to feel that people might be watching him and trying to detect something. This conscious expression, since it was as far as possible from boyish mirthfulness, was usually attributed to insolence or "smartness."

As the inquisition proceeded, one of his instructors repeated an impertinent remark of the boy's, and the Principal asked him whether he thought that a courteous speech to make to a woman. Paul grinned and said he guessed so. When he was told that he could go, he bowed gracefully and went out. His bow was like a repetition of the scandalous red carnation.

His teachers were in despair, and his drawing-master voiced the feeling of them all when he declared there was something about the boy which none of them understood. He added: "I don't really believe that smile of his comes altogether from insolence; there's something sort of haunted about it. The boy is not strong, for one thing. There is something wrong about the fellow."

The drawing-master had come to realize that, in looking at Paul, one saw only his white teeth and the forced animation of his eyes. One warm afternoon the boy had gone to sleep at his drawing-board, and his master had noted with amazement what a white, blue-veined face it was; drawn and wrinkled like an old man's about the eyes, the lips twitching even in his sleep.

His teachers left the building dissatisfied and unhappy; humiliated to have felt so vindictive toward a mere boy, to have uttered this feeling in cutting terms, and to have set each other on, as it were, in the gruesome game of intemperate reproach. One of them remembered having seen a miserable street cat set at bay by a ring of tormentors.

As for Paul, he ran down the hill whistling the Soldiers' Chorus from "Faust," looking behind him now and then to see whether some of his teachers were not there to witness his light-heartedness. As it was now late in the afternoon and Paul was on duty that evening as usher at Carnegie Hall, he decided that he would not go home to supper.

When he reached the concert hall, the doors were not yet open. It was chilly outside, and he decided to go up into the picture gallery—always deserted at this hour—where there were some of Raffelli's gay studies of Paris streets and an airy blue Venetian scene or two that always exhilarated him. He was delighted to find no one in the gallery but the old guard, who sat in the corner, a newspaper on his knee, a black patch over one eye and the other closed. Paul possessed himself of the place and walked confidently up and down, whistling under his breath. After a while he sat down before a blue Rico and lost himself.

When he bethought him to look at his watch, it was after seven o'clock, and he rose with a start and ran downstairs, making a face at Augustus Caesar, peering out from the cast-room and an evil gesture at the Venus of Milo as he passed her on the stairway.

When Paul reached the ushers' dressing-room, half a dozen boys were there already, and he began excitedly to tumble into his uniform. It was one of the few that at all approached fitting, and Paul thought it very becoming—though he knew the tight, straight coat accentuated his narrow chest, about which he was exceedingly sensitive. He was always excited while he dressed, twanging all over to the tuning of the strings and the preliminary flourishes of the horns in the music-room; but tonight he seemed quite beside himself, and he teased and plagued the boys until, telling him that he was crazy, they put him down on the floor and sat on him.

Somewhat calmed by his suppression, Paul dashed out to the front of the house to seat the early comers. He was a model usher. Gracious and smiling he ran up and down the aisles. Nothing was too much trouble for him; he carried messages and brought programmes as though it were his greatest pleasure in life, and all the people in his section thought him a charming boy, feeling that he remembered and admired them. As the house filled, he grew more and more vivacious and animated, and the colour came to his cheeks and lips. It was very much as though this were a great reception and Paul were the host. Just as the musicians came out to take their places, his English teacher arrived with cheques for the seats which a prominent manufacturer had taken for the season. She betrayed some embarrassment when she handed Paul the tickets, and a hauteur which subsequently made her feel very foolish. Paul was startled for a moment, and had the feeling of wanting to put her out; what business had she here among all these fine people and gay colours? He looked her over and decided that she was not appropriately dressed and must be a fool to sit downstairs in such togs. The tickets had probably been sent her out of kindness, he reflected, as he put down a seat for her, and she had about as much right to sit there as he had.

When the symphony began, Paul sank into one of the rear seats with a long sigh of relief, and lost himself as he had done before the Rico. It was not that symphonies, as such, meant anything in particular to Paul, but the first sight of the instruments seemed to free some hilarious spirit within him; something that struggled there like the genie in the bottle found by the Arab fisherman. He felt a sudden zest of life; the lights danced before his eyes and the concert hall blazed into unimaginable splendour. When the soprano soloist came on, Paul forgot even the nastiness of his teacher's being there, and gave himself up to the peculiar intoxication such personages always had for him. The soloist chanced to be a German woman, by no means in her first youth, and the mother of many children; but she wore a satin gown and a tiara, and she had that indefinable air of achievement, the world-shine upon her, which always blinded Paul to any possible defects.

After a concert was over, Paul was often irritable and wretched until he got to sleep—and tonight he was even more than usually restless. He had the feeling of not being able to let down; of its being impossible to give up this delicious excitement which was the only thing that could be called living at all. During the last number he withdrew and, after hastily changing his clothes in the dressing-room, slipped out to the side door where the singer's carriage stood. Here he began pacing rapidly up and down the walk, waiting to see her come out.

Over yonder the Schenley, in its vacant stretch, loomed big and square through the fine rain, the windows of its twelve stories glowing like those of a lighted cardboard house under a Christmas tree. All the actors and singers of any importance stayed there when they were in Pittsburgh, and a number of the big manufacturers of the place lived there in the winter. Paul had often hung about the hotel, watching the people go in and out, longing to enter and leave schoolmasters and dull care behind him forever.

At last the singer came out, accompanied by the conductor, who helped her into her carriage and closed the door with a cordial *auf wiedersehen*—which set Paul to wondering whether she were not an old sweetheart of his. Paul followed the carriage over to the hotel, walking so rapidly as not to be far from the entrance when the singer alighted and disappeared behind the swinging glass doors which were opened by a Negro in a tall hat and a long coat. In the moment that the door was ajar, it seemed to Paul that he, too, entered. He seemed to feel himself go after her up the steps, into the warm lighted building, into an exotic, a tropical world of shiny, glistening surfaces and basking ease. He reflected upon the mysterious dishes that were brought into the dining room, the green bottles in buckets of ice, as he had seen them in the supper-party pictures of the Sunday supplement. A quick gust of wind brought the rain down with sudden vehemence, and Paul was startled to find that he was still outside in the slush of the gravel driveway; that his boots were letting in the water and his scanty overcoat was clinging wet about him; that the lights in front of the concert hall were out, and that the rain was driving in sheets between him and the orange glow of the windows above him. There it was, what he wanted—tangible before him, like the fairy world of a Christmas pantomime; as the rain beat in his face, Paul wondered whether he were destined always to shiver in the black night outside, looking up at it.

He turned and walked reluctantly toward the car tracks. The end had to come sometime; his father in his night-clothes at the top of the stairs, explanations that did not explain, hastily improvised fictions that were forever tripping him up, his upstairs room and its horrible yellow wallpaper, the creaking bureau with the greasy plush collar-box and over his painted wooden bed the pictures of George Washington and John Calvin, and the framed motto, "Feed my Lambs," which had been worked in red worsted by his mother, who Paul could not remember.

Half an hour later, Paul alighted from the Negley Avenue car and went slowly down one of the side streets off the main thoroughfare. It was a highly respectable street, where all the houses were exactly alike, and where business men of moderate means begot and reared large families of children, all of who went to Sabbath School and learned the shorter catechism, and were interested in arithmetic; all of whom were as exactly alike as their homes, and of a piece with the monotony in which they lived. Paul never went up Cordelia Street without a shudder of loathing. His home was next to the house of the Cumberland minister. He approached it tonight with the nerveless sense of defeat, the hopeless feeling of sinking back forever into ugliness and commonness that he had always had when he came home. The moment he turned into Cordelia Street he felt the waters close above his head. After each of these orgies of living, he experienced all the physical depression which follows a debauch; the loathing of respectable beds, of common food, of a house permeated by kitchen odours; a shuddering repulsion for the flavourless, colourless mass of everyday existence; a morbid desire for cool things and soft lights and fresh flowers.

The nearer he approached the house, the more absolutely unequal Paul felt to the sight of it all: his ugly sleeping chamber; the old bathroom with the grimy zinc tub, the cracked mirror, the dripping spigots; his father, at the top of the stairs, his hairy legs sticking out from his nightshirt, his feet thrust into carpet slippers. He was so much later than usual that there would certainly be enquiries and reproaches. Paul stopped short before the door. He felt that he could not be accosted by his father tonight; that he could not toss again on that miserable bed. He would not go in. He would tell his father that he had no carfare, and it was raining so hard he had gone home with one of the boys and stayed all night.

Meanwhile, he was wet and cold. He went around to the back of the house and tried one of the basement windows, found it open, raised it cautiously, and scrambled down the cellar wall to the floor. There he stood, holding his breath, terrified by the noise he had made; but the floor above him was silent, and there was no creak on the stairs. He found a soap-box, and carried it over to the soft ring of light that streamed from the furnace door, and sat down. He was horribly afraid of rats, so he did not try to sleep but sat looking distrustfully at the dark, still terrified lest he might have awakened his father.

In such reactions, after one of the experiences which made days and nights out of the dreary blanks of the calendar, when his senses were deadened, Paul's head was always singularly clear. Suppose his father had heard him getting in at the window and had come down and shot him for a burglar? Then, again, suppose his father had come down, pistol in hand, and he had cried out in time to save himself, and his father had been horrified to think how nearly he had killed him? Then again, suppose a day should come when his father would remember that night, and wish there had been no warning cry to stay his hand? With this last supposition Paul entertained himself until daybreak.

The following Sunday was fine; the sodden November chill was broken by the last flash of autumnal summer. In the morning Paul had to go to church and Sabbath School, as always. On seasonable Sunday afternoons the burghers of Cordelia Street usually sat out on their front stoops and talked to their neighbours on the next stoop, or called to those across the street in neighbourly fashion. The men sat placidly on gay cushions placed upon the steps that led down to the sidewalk, while the women, in their Sunday "waists," sat in rockers on the cramped porches, pretending to be greatly at their ease. The children played in the streets; there were so many of them that the place resembled the recreation grounds of a kindergarten. The men on the steps, all in their shirt-sleeves, their vests unbuttoned, sat with their legs well apart, their stomachs comfortably protruding, and talked of the prices of this, or told anecdotes of the sagacity of their various chiefs and overlords. They occasionally looked over the multitude of squabbling children, listened affectionately to their high-pitched, nasal voices, smiling to see their own proclivities reproduced in their offspring, and interspersed their legends of the iron kings with remarks about their sons' progress at school, their grades in arithmetic, and the amounts they had saved in their toy banks.

On this last Sunday of November, Paul sat all the afternoon on the lowest step of his stoop, staring into the street, while his sisters, in their rockers, were talking to the minister's daughters next door about how many shirtwaists they had made in the last week, and how many waffles someone had eaten at the last church supper. When the weather was warm, and his father was in a particularly jovial frame of mind, the girls made lemonade, which was always brought out in a red-glass pitcher, ornamented with forget-me-nots in blue enamel. This the girls thought very fine, and the neighbors joked about the suspicious colour of the pitcher.

Today Paul's father, on the top step, was talking to a young man who shifted a restless baby from knee to knee. He happened to be the young man who was daily held up to Paul as a model, and after whom it was his father's dearest hope that he would pattern. This young man was of a ruddy complexion, with a compressed, red mouth, and faded, nearsighted eyes, over which he wore thick spectacles, with gold bows that curved about his ears. He was clerk to one of the magnates of a great steel corporation, and was looked upon in Cordelia Street as a young man with a future. There was a story that, some five years ago—he was now barely twenty-six—he had been a trifle "dissipated," but in order to curb his appetites and save the loss of time and strength that a sowing of wild oats might have entailed, he had taken his chief's advice, oft reiterated to his employees, and at twenty-one had married the first woman whom he could persuade to share his fortunes. She happened to be an angular schoolmistress, much older than he, who also wore thick glasses, and who had now borne him four children, all nearsighted like herself.

The young man was relating how his chief, now cruising in the Mediterranean, kept in touch with all the details of the business, arranging his office house on his yacht just as though he were at home, and "knocking off work enough to keep two stenographers busy." His father told, in turn, the plan his corporation was considering, of putting in a electric railway plant at Cairo. Paul snapped his teeth; he had an awful apprehension that they might spoil it all before he got there. Yet he rather liked to hear these legends of the iron kings, that were told and retold on Sundays and holidays; these stories of palaces in Venice, yachts on the Mediterranean, and high play at Monte Carlo appealed to his fancy, and he was interested in the triumphs of cash-boys who had become famous, though he had no mind for the cash-boy stage.

After supper was over, and he had helped to dry the dishes, Paul nervously asked his father whether he could go to George's to get some help in his geometry, and still more nervously asked for carfare. This latter request he had to repeat, as his father, on principle, did not like to hear requests for money, whether much or little. He asked Paul whether he could not go to some boy who lived nearer, and told him that he ought not to leave his school work until Sunday; but he gave him the dime. He was not a poor man, but he had a worthy ambition to come up in the world. His only reason for allowing Paul to usher was that he thought a boy ought to be earning a little.

Paul bounded upstairs, scrubbed the greasy odour of the dishwater from his hands with the ill-smelling soap he hated, and then shook over his fingers a few drops of violet water from the bottle he kept hidden in his drawer. He left the house with his geometry conspicuously under his arm, and the moment he got out of Cordelia Street and boarded a downtown car, he shook off the lethargy of two deadening days, and began to live again.

The leading juvenile of the permanent stock company which played at one of the downtown theatres was an acquaintance of Paul's, and the boy had been invited to drop in at the Sunday-night rehearsals whenever he could. For more that a year Paul had spent every available moment loitering about Charley Edwards's dressing-room. He had won a place among Edwards's following not only because the young actor, who could not afford to employ a dresser, often found him useful, but because he recognized in Paul something akin to what churchmen term "vocation."

It was at the theatre and at Carnegie Hall that Paul really lived; the rest was but a sleep and a forgetting. This was Paul's fairy tale, and it had for him all the allurement of a secret love. The moment he inhaled the gassy, painty, dusty odour behind the scenes, he breathed like a prisoner set free, and felt within him the possibility of doing or saying splendid, brilliant things. The moment the cracked orchestra beat out the overture from "Martha," or jerked at the serenade from "Rigoletto," all stupid and ugly things slid from him, and his senses were deliciously, yet delicately fired.

Perhaps it was because, in Paul's world, the natural nearly always wore the guise of ugliness, that a certain element of artificiality seemed to him necessary in beauty. Perhaps it was because his experience of life elsewhere was so full of Sabbath-School picnics, petty economics, wholesome advice as to how to succeed in life, and the unescapable odours of cooking, that he found this existence so alluring, these smartly clad men and women so attractive, that he was so moved by these starry apple orchards that bloomed perennially under the limelight. It would be difficult to put it strongly enough how convincingly the stage entrance of that theatre was for Paul the actual portal of Romance. Certainly none of the company ever suspected it, least of all Charley Edwards. It was very like the old stories that used to float about London of fabulously rich Jews, who had subterranean halls, with palms, and fountains, and soft lamps and richly apparelled women who never saw the disenchanting light of London day. So, in the midst of that smoke-palled city, enamoured of figures and grimy toil, Paul had his secret temple, his wishing-carpet, his bit of blue-and-white Mediterranean shore bathed in perpetual sunshine.

Several of Paul's teachers had a theory that his imagination had been perverted by garish fiction; but the truth was he scarcely ever read at all. The books at home were not such as would either tempt or corrupt a youthful mind, and as for reading the novels that some of his friends urged upon him—well, he got what he wanted much more quickly from music; any sort of music, from an orchestra to a barrel-organ. He needed only the spark, the indescribable thrill that made his imagination master of his senses, and he could make plots and pictures enough of his own. It was equally true that he was not stage-struck—not, at any rate, in the usual acceptation of that expression. He had no desire to become an actor, any more than he had to become a musician. He felt no necessity to do any of these things; what he wanted was to see, to be in the atmosphere, float on the wave of it, to be carried out, blue league after league, away from everything.

After a night behind the scenes, Paul found the schoolroom more than ever repulsive; the bare floors and naked walls; the prosy men who never wore frock coats, or violets in their buttonholes; the women with their dull gowns, shrill voices, and pitiful seriousness about prepositions that govern the dative. He could not bear to have the other pupils think, for a moment, that he took these people seriously; he must convey to them that he considered it all trivial, and was there only by way of a joke, anyway. He had autographed pictures of all the members of the stock company which he showed his classmates, telling them the most incredible stories of his familiarity with these people, of his acquaintance with the soloists who came to Carnegie Hall, his suppers with them and the flowers he sent them. When these stories lost their effect, and the audience grew listless, he would bid all the boys goodbye, announcing that he was going to travel for a while; going to Naples, to California, to Egypt. Then, next Monday, he would slip back, conscious and nervously smiling; his sister was ill, and he would have to defer his voyage until spring.

Matters went steadily worse with Paul at school. In the itch to let his instructors know how heartily he despised them, and how thoroughly he was appreciated elsewhere, he mentioned once or twice that he had no time to fool with theorems; adding—with a twitch of the eyebrows and a touch of that nervous bravado which so perplexed them—that he was helping the people down at the stock company; they were old friends of his.

The upshot of the matter was that the Principal went to Paul's father, and Paul was taken out of school and put to work. The manager at Carnegie Hall was told to get another usher in his stead; the doorkeeper at the theatre was warned not to admit him to the house; and Charley Edwards remorsefully promised the boy's father not to see him again.

The members of the stock company were vastly amused when some of Paul's stories reached them—especially the women. They were hard-working women, most of them supporting indolent husbands or brothers, and they laughed rather bitterly at having stirred the boy to such fervid and florid inventions. They agreed with the faculty and with his father, that Paul's was a bad case.

The east-bound train was ploughing through a January snowstorm; the dull dawn was beginning to show grey when the engine whistled a mile out of Newark. Paul started up from the seat where he had lain curled in uneasy slumber, rubbed the breath-misted window-glass with his hand, and peered out. The snow was whirling in curling eddies above the white bottom lands, and the drifts lay already deep in the fields and along the fences, while here and there the tall dead grass and dried weed stalks protruded black about it. Lights shone from the scattered houses, and a gang of labourers who stood beside the track waved their lanterns.

Paul had slept very little, and he felt grimy and uncomfortable. He had made the all-night journey in a day coach because he was afraid if he took a Pullman he might be seen by some Pittsburgh business man who had noticed him in Denny and Carson's office. When the whistle woke him, he clutched quickly at his breast pocket, glancing about him with an uncertain smile. But the little, clay-bespattered Italians were still sleeping, the slatternly women across the aisle were in open-mouthed oblivion, and even the crumby, crying babies were for the time stilled. Paul settled back to struggle with his impatience as best he could.

When he arrived at the Jersey City station, he hurried through his breakfast, manifestly ill at ease and keeping a sharp eye about him. After he reached the Twenty-Third Street station, he consulted a cabman, and had himself driven to a men's furnishing establishment which was just opening for the day. He spent upward of two hours there, buying with endless reconsidering and great care. The new street suit he put on in the fitting-room; the frock coat and dress clothes he had bundled into the cab with his new shirts. Then he drove to a hatter's and a shoe house. His next errand was at Tiffany's, where he selected silver-mounted brushes and a scarf-pin. He would not wait to have his silver marked, he said.

Lastly, he stopped at a trunk shop on Broadway, and had his purchases packed into various travelling bags.

It was a little after one o'clock when he drove up to the Waldorf, and, after settling with the cabman, went into the office. He registered from Washington; said his mother and father had been abroad, and that he had come down to await the arrival of their steamer. He told his story plausibly and had no trouble, since he offered to pay for them in advance, in engaging his rooms; a sleeping room, sitting-room, and bath.

Not once, but a hundred times Paul had planned this entry into New York. He had gone over every detail of it with Charley Edwards, and in his scrapbook at home there were pages of description about New York hotels, cut from the Sunday papers.

When he was shown to his sitting-room on the eighth floor, he saw at a glance that everything was as it should be; there was but one detail in his mental picture that the place did not realize, so he rang for the bell-boy and sent him down for flowers. He moved about nervously until the boy returned, putting away his linen and fingering it delightedly as he did so. When the flowers came, he put them hastily into water, and then tumbled into a hot bath. Presently he came out of his white bathroom, resplendent in his new silk underwear, and playing with the tassels of his red robe. The snow was whirling so fiercely outside his windows that he could scarcely see across the street; but within, the air was deliciously soft and fragrant. He put the violets and jonquils on the tabouret beside the couch, and threw himself down with a long sigh, covering himself with a Roman blanket. He was thoroughly tired; he had been in such haste, he had stood up to such a strain, covered so much ground in the last twenty-four hours, that he wanted to think how it had all come about. Lulled by the sound of the wind, the warm air, and the cool fragrance of the flowers, he sank into deep, drowsy retrospection.

It had been wonderfully simple; when they had shut him out of theatre and concert hall, when they had taken away his bone, the whole thing was virtually determined. The rest was a mere matter of opportunity. The only thing that at all surprised him was his own courage—for he realized well enough that he had always been tormented by fear, a sort of apprehensive dread which, of late years, as the meshes of the lies he had told closed about him, had been pulling the muscles of his body tighter and tighter. Until now, he could not remember a time when he had not been dreading something. Even when he was a little boy, it was always there—behind him, or before, or on either side. There had always been the shadowed corner, the dark place into which he dared not look, but from which something seemed always to be watching him—and Paul had done things that were not pretty to watch, he knew.

But now he had a curious sense of relief, as though he had at last thrown down the gauntlet to the thing in the corner.

Yet it was but a day since he had been sulking in the traces; but yesterday afternoon that he had been sent to the bank with Denny and Carson's deposit, as usual—but this time he was instructed to leave the book to be balanced. There was above two thousand dollars in checks, and nearly a thousand in the bank notes which he had taken from the book and quietly transferred to his pocket. At the bank he had made out a new deposit slip. His nerves had been steady enough to permit of his returning to the office, where he had finished his work and asked for a full day's holiday tomorrow, Saturday, giving a perfectly reasonable pretext. The bank book, he knew, would not be returned before Monday or Tuesday, and his father would be out of town for the next week. From the time he slipped the bank notes into his pocket until he boarded the night train for New York, he had not known a moment's hesitation.

How astonishingly easy it had all been; here he was, the thing done; and this time there would be no awakening, no figure at the top of the stairs. He watched the snow flakes whirling by his window until he fell asleep.

When he awoke, it was four o'clock in the afternoon. He bounded up with a start; one of his precious days gone already! He spent nearly an hour in dressing, watching every stage of his toilet carefully in the mirror. Everything was quite perfect; he was exactly the kind of boy he had always wanted to be.

When he went downstairs, Paul took a carriage and drove up Fifth Avenue toward the park. The snow had somewhat abated; carriages and tradesman's wagons were hurrying soundlessly to and fro in the winter twilight; boys in woolen mufflers were shovelling off the doorsteps; the avenue stages made fine spots of colour against the white street. Here and there on the corners whole flower gardens blooming behind glass windows, against which the snow flakes stuck and melted; violets, roses, carnations, lilies of the valley—somehow vastly more lovely and alluring that they blossomed thus unnaturally in the snow. The Park itself was a wonderful stage winter-piece.

When he returned, the pause of the twilight had ceased, and the tune of the streets had changed. The snow was falling faster, lights streamed from the hotels that reared their many stories fearlessly up into the storm, defying the raging Atlantic winds. A long, black stream of carriages poured down the avenue, intersected here and there by other streams, tending horizontally. There were a score of cabs about the entrance of this hotel, and his driver had to wait. Boys in livery were running in and out of the awning stretched across the sidewalk, up and down the red velvet carpet laid from the door to the street. Above, about, within it all, was the rumble and roar, the hurry and toss of thousands of human beings as hot for pleasure as himself, and on every side of him towered the glaring affirmation of the omnipotence of wealth.

The boy set his teeth and drew his shoulders together in a spasm of realization; the plot of all dramas, and text of all romances, the nerve-stuff of all sensations was whirling about him like the snow flakes. He burnt like a faggot in a tempest.

When Paul came down to dinner, the music of the orchestra floated up the elevator shaft to greet him. As he stepped into the thronged corridor, he sank back into one of the chairs against the wall to get his breath. The lights, the chatter, the perfumes, the bewildering medley of colour—he had, for a moment, the feeling of not being able to stand it. But only for a moment; these were his own people, he told himself. He went slowly about the corridors, through the writing-rooms, reception-rooms, as though he were exploring the chambers of an enchanted palace, built and peopled for him alone.

When he reached the dining-room he sat down at a table near a window. The flowers, the white linen, the many-coloured wine glasses, the gay toilettes of the women, the low popping of corks, the undulating repetitions of the Blue Danube from the orchestra, all flooded Paul's dream with bewildering radiance. When the roseate tinge of his champagne was added—that cold, precious, bubbling stuff that creamed and foamed in his glass—Paul wondered that there were honest men in the world at all. This was what all the world was fighting for, he reflected; this was what all the struggle was about. He doubted the reality of his past. Had he ever known a place called Cordelia Street, a place where fagged looking business men boarded the early car? Mere rivets in a machine they seemed to Paul, sickening men, with combings of children's hair always hanging to their coats, and the smell of cooking in their clothes. Cordelia Street—Ah, that belonged to another time and country! Had he not always been thus, had he not sat here night after night, from as far back as he could remember, looking pensively over just such shimmering textures, and slowly twirling the stem of a glass like this one between his thumb and middle finger? He rather thought he had.

He was not in the least abashed or lonely. He had no special desire to meet or to know any of these people; all he demanded was the right to look on and conjecture, to watch the pageant. The mere stage properties were all he contended for. Nor was he lonely later in the evening, in his loge at the Opera. He was entirely rid of his nervous misgivings, of his forced aggressiveness, of the imperative desire to show himself different from his surroundings. He felt now that his surrounding explained him. Nobody questioned the purple, he had only to wear it passively. He had only to glance down at his dress coat to reassure himself that here it would be impossible for anyone to humiliate him.

He found it hard to leave his beautiful sitting-room to go to bed that night, and sat long watching the raging storm from his turret window. When he went to sleep, it was with the lights turned on in his bedroom; partly because of his old timidity, and partly so that, if he should wake in the night, there would be no wretched moment of doubt, no horrible suspicion of yellow wall-paper, or of Washington and Calvin above his bed.

On Sunday morning the city was practically snow-bound. Paul breakfasted late, and in the afternoon he fell in with a wild San Francisco boy, a freshman at Yale, who said he had run down for a "little flyer" over Sunday. The young man offered to show Paul the night side of the town, and the two boys went off together after dinner, not returning to the hotel until seven o'clock the next morning. They had started out in the confiding warmth of a champagne friendship, but their parting in the elevator was singularly cool. The freshman pulled himself together to make his train, and Paul went to bed. He awoke at two o'clock in the afternoon, very thirsty and dizzy, and rang for ice-water, coffee, and the Pittsburgh papers.

On the part of the hotel management, Paul excited no suspicion. There was this to be said for him, that he wore his spoils with dignity and in no way made himself conspicuous. His chief greediness lay in his ears and eyes, and his excesses were not offensive ones. His dearest pleasures were the grey winter twilights in his sitting-room; his quiet enjoyment of his flowers, his clothes, his wide divan, his cigarette and his sense of power. He could not remember a time when he had felt so at peace with himself. The mere release from the necessity of petty lying, lying every day and every day, restored his self-respect. He had never lied for pleasure, even at school; but to make himself noticed and admired, to assert his difference from the other Cordelia Street boys; and he felt a good deal more manly, more honest, even, now that he had no need for boastful pretensions, now that he could, as his actor friends used to say, "dress the part." It was characteristic that remorse did not occur to him. His golden days went by without a shadow, and he made each as perfect as he could.

On the eighth day after his arrival in New York, he found the whole affair exploited in the Pittsburgh papers, exploited with a wealth of detail which indicated that local news of a sensational nature was at a low ebb. The firm of Denny & Carson announced that the boy's father had refunded the full amount of his theft, and that they had no intention of prosecuting. The Cumberland minister had been interviewed, and expressed his hope of yet reclaiming the motherless lad, and Paul's Sabbath-school teacher declared that she would spare no effort to that end. The rumour had reached Pittsburgh that the boy had been seen in a New York hotel, and his father had gone East to find him and bring him home.

Paul had just come in to dress for dinner; he sank into a chair, weak in the knees, and clasped his head in his hands. It was to be worse than jail, even; the tepid waters of Cordelia Street were to close over him finally and forever. The grey monotony stretched before him in hopeless, unrelieved years; Sabbath-school, Young People's Meeting, the yellow-papered room, the damp dish-towels; it all rushed back upon him with sickening vividness. He had the old feeling that the orchestra had suddenly stopped, the sinking sensation that the play was over. The sweat broke out on his face and he sprang to his feet, looked about him with his white, conscious smile, and winked at himself in the mirror. With something of the childish belief in miracles with which he had so often gone to class, all his lessons unlearned, Paul dressed and dashed whistling down the corridor to the elevator.

He had no sooner entered the dining-room and caught the measure of the music, than his remembrance was lightened by his old elastic power of claiming the moment, mounting with it, and finding it all sufficient. The glare and glitter about him, the mere scenic accessories had again, and for the last time, their old potency. He would show himself that he was game, he would finish the thing splendidly.

He doubted, more than ever, the existence of Cordelia Street, and for the first time he drank his wine recklessly. Was he not, after all, one of these fortunate beings? He drummed a nervous accompaniment to the music and looked about him, telling himself over and over that it had paid. He reflected drowsily, to the swell of the violin and the chill sweetness of his wine, that he might have done it more wisely. He might have caught an outbound steamer and been well out of their clutches before now. But the other side of the world had seemed too far away and too uncertain then; he could not have waited for it; his need had been too sharp. If he had to choose over again, he would do the same thing tomorrow. He looked affectionately about the dining-room, now gilded with soft mist. Ah, it had paid indeed!

Paul was awakened next morning by a painful throbbing in his head and feet. He had thrown himself across the bed without undressing, and had slept with his shoes on. His limbs and hands were lead heavy, and his tongue and throat were parched. There came upon him one of those fateful attacks of clear-headedness that never occurred except when he was physically exhausted and his nerves hung loose. He lay still and closed his eyes and let the tide of realities wash over him.

His father was in New York; "Stopping at some joint or other," he told himself. The memory of successive summers on the front stoop fell upon him like a weight of black water. He had not a hundred dollars left; and he knew now, more than ever, that money was everything, the wall that stood between all he loathed and all he wanted. The thing was winding itself up; he had thought of that on his first glorious day in New York, and had even provided a way to snap the thread. It lay on his dressing-table now; he had it out last night when he came blindly up from dinner—but the shiny metal hurt his eyes, and he disliked the look of it, anyway.

He rose and moved about with a painful effort, succumbing now and again to attacks of nausea. It was the old depression exaggerated; all the world had become Cordelia Street. Yet somehow he was not afraid of anything, was absolutely calm; perhaps because he had looked into the dark corner at last, and knew. It was bad enough, what he saw there; but somehow not so bad as his long fear of it had been. He saw everything clearly now. He had a feeling that he had made the best of it, that he had lived the sort of life he was meant to live, and for half an hour he sat staring at the revolver. But he told himself that was not the way, so he went downstairs and took a cab to the ferry.

When Paul arrived at Newark, he got off the train and took another cab, directing the driver to follow the Pennsylvania tracks out of the town. The snow lay heavy on the roadways and had drifted deep in the open fields. Only here and there the dead grass or dried weed stalks projected, singularly black, above it. Once well into the country, Paul dismissed the carriage and walked, floundering along the tracks, his mind a medley of irrelevant things. He seemed to hold in his brain an actual picture of everything he had seen that morning. He remembered every feature of both his drivers, the toothless old woman from whom he had bought the red flowers in his coat, the agent from whom he had got his ticket, and all of his fellow-passengers on the ferry. His mind, unable to cope with vital matters near at hand, worked feverishly and deftly at sorting and grouping these images. They made for him a part of the ugliness of the world, of the ache in his head, and the bitter burning on his tongue. He stooped and put a handful of.snow into his mouth as he walked, but that, too. seemed hot. When he reached a little hillside, where the tracks ran through cut some twenty feet below him, he stopped and sat down.

The carnations in his coat were drooping with the cold, he noticed; all their red glory over. It occurred to him that all the flowers he had seen in the show windows that first night must have gone the same way, long before this. It was only one splendid breath they had, in spite of their brave mockery at the winter outside the glass. It was a losing game in the end, it seemed, this revolt against the homilies by which the world is run. Paul took one of the blossoms carefully from his coat and scooped a little hole in the snow, where he covered it up. Then he dozed a while, from his weak condition, seeming insensible to the cold.

The sound of an approaching train woke him, and he started to his feet, remembering only his resolution, and afraid lest he should be too late. He stood watching the approaching locomotive, his teeth chattering, his lips drawn away from them in a frightened smile; once or twice he glanced nervously sidewise, as though he were being watched. When the right moment came, he jumped. As he fell, the folly of his haste occurred to him with merciless clearness, the vastness of what he had left undone. There flashed through his brain, clearer than ever before, the blue of Adriatic water, the yellow of Algerian sands.

He felt something strike his chest—his body was being thrown swiftly through the air, on and on, immeasurably far and fast, while his limbs gently relaxed. Then, because the picture making mechanism was crushed, and disturbing visions flashed into black, Paul dropped back into the immense design of things.

TOM'S HUSBAND

Sarah Orne Jewett

I shall not dwell long upon the circumstances that led to the marriage of my hero and heroine; though their courtship was to them, the only one that has ever noticeably approached the ideal, it had many aspects in which it was entirely commonplace in other people's eyes. While the world in general smiles at lovers with kindly approval and sympathy, it refuses to be aware of the unprecedented delight which is amazing to the lovers themselves.

But as has been true in many other cases, when they were at last married, the most ideal of situations was found to have been changed to the most practical. Instead of having shared their original duties, and, as school-boys would say, going halves, they discovered that the cares of life had been doubled. This led to some distressing moments for both our friends; they understood suddenly that instead of dwelling in heaven they were still upon earth, and had made themselves slaves to new laws and limitations. Instead of being freer and happier than ever before, they had assumed new responsibilities; they had established a new household, and must fulfill in some way or another the obligations of it. They looked back with affection to their engagement; they had been longing to have each other to themselves, apart from the world, but it seemed that they never felt so keenly that they were still units in modern society. Since Adam and Eve were in Paradise, before the devil joined them, nobody has had a chance to imitate that unlucky couple. In some respects they told the truth when, twenty times a day, they said that it had never been so pleasant before; but there were mental reservations on either side which might have subjected them to the accusation of lying. Somehow, there was a little feeling of disappointment, and they caught themselves wondering—though they would have died sooner than confess it—whether they were quite so happy as they had expected. The truth was, they were much happier than people usually are, for they had an uncommon capacity for enjoyment. For a little while they were like a sailboat that is beating and has to drift a few minutes before it can catch the wind and start off on the other tack. And they had the same feeling, too, that any one is likely to have who has been long pursuing some object of his ambition or desire. Whether it is a coin, or a picture, or a stray volume of some old edition of Shakespeare, or whether it is an office under government or a lover, when fairly in one's grasp there is a loss of the eagerness that was felt in pursuit. Satisfaction, even after one has dined well, is not so interesting and eager a feeling as hunger.

My hero and heroine were reasonably well established to begin with: they each had some money, though Mr. Wilson had most. His father had at one time been a rich man, but with the decline, a few years before, of manufacturing interests, he had become, mostly through the fault of others, somewhat involved; and at the time of his death his affairs were in such a condition that it was still a question whether a very large sum or moderately large one would represent his estate. Mrs. Wilson, Tom's step-mother, was somewhat of an invalid; she suffered severely at times with asthma, but she was almost entirely relieved by living in another part of the country. While her husband lived, she had accepted her illness as inevitable, and rarely left home; but during the last few years she had lived in Philadelphia with her own people, making short and wheezing visits only from time to time, and had not undergone a voluntary period of suffering since the occasion of Tom's marriage, which she had entirely approved. She had sufficient property of her own, and she and Tom were independent of each other in that way. Her only other step-child was a daughter, who had married a navy officer, and had at this time gone out to spend three years (or less) with her husband, who had been ordered to Japan.

It is not infrequently noticed that in many marriages one of the persons who choose each other as partners for life is said to have thrown himself or herself away, and the relatives and friends look on with dismal forebodings and ill-concealed submission. In this case it was the wife who might have done so much better, according to public opinion. She did not think so herself, luckily, either before marriage or afterward, and I do not think it occurred to her to picture to herself the sort of career which would have been her alternative. She had been an only child, and had usually taken her own way. Someone once said that it was a great pity that she had not been obliged to work for her living, for she had inherited a most uncommon business talent, and, without being disreputably keen at a bargain, her insight into the practical working of affairs was very clear and far-reaching. Her father, who had also been a manufacturer, like Tom's, had often said it had been a mistake that she was a girl instead of a boy. Such executive ability as hers is often wasted in the more contracted sphere of women, and is apt to be more a disadvantage than a help. She was too independent and self-reliant for a wife; it would seem at first thought that she needed a wife herself more than she did a husband. Most men like best the women whose natures cling and appeal to theirs for protection. But Tom Wilson, while he did not wish to be protected himself, liked these very qualities in his wife which would have displeased some other men; to tell the truth, he was very much in love with his wife just as she was. He was a successful collector of almost everything but money, and during a great part of his life he had been an invalid, and he had grown, as he laughingly confessed, very old-womanish. He had been badly lamed, when a boy, by being caught in some machinery in his father's mill, near which he was idling one afternoon, and though he had almost entirely outgrown the effect of his injury, it had not been until after many years. He had been in college, but his eyes had given out there, and he had been obliged to leave in the middle of his junior year, though he had kept up a pleasant intercourse with the members of his class, with whom he had been a great favorite. He was a good deal of an idler in the world. I do not think his ambition, except in the case of securing Mary Dunn for his wife, had ever been distinct; he seemed to make the most he could of each day as it came, without making all his days' works tend toward some grand result, and go toward the upbuilding of some grand plan and purpose. He consequently gave no promise of being either distinguished or great. When his eyes would allow, he was an indefatigable reader; and although he would have said that he read only for amusement, yet he amused himself with books that were well worth the time he spent over them.

The house where he lived nominally belonged to his step-mother, but she had taken for granted that Tom would bring his wife home to it, and assured him that it should be to all intents and purposes his. Tom was deeply attached to the old place, which was altogether the pleasantest in town. He had kept bachelor's hall there most of the time since his father's death, and he had taken great pleasure, before his marriage, in refitting it to some extent, though it was already comfortable and furnished in remarkably good taste. People said of him that if it had not been for his illnesses, and if he had been a poor boy, he probably would have made something of himself. As it was, he was not very well known by the townspeople, being somewhat reserved, and not taking much interest in their every-day subjects of conversation. Nobody liked him so well as they liked his wife, yet there was no reason why he should be disliked enough to have much said about him.

After our friends had been married for some time, and had outlived the first strangeness of the new order of things, and had done their duty to their neighbors with so much apparent willingness and generosity that even Tom himself was liked a great deal better than he ever had been before, they were sitting together one stormy evening in the library, before the fire. Mrs. Wilson had been reading Tom the letters which had come to him by the night's mail. There was a long one from his sister in Nagasaki, which had been written with a good deal of ill-disguised reproach. She complained of the smallness of the income of her share in her father's estate, and said that she had been assured by American friends that the smaller mills were starting up everywhere, and beginning to do well again. Four per cent on her other property, which she had been told she must soon expect instead of eight, would make a great difference to her. A navy captain in a foreign port was obliged to entertain a great deal, and Tom must know that it cost them much more to live than it did him, and ought to think of their interests. She hoped he would talk over what was best to be done with their mother (who had been made executor, with Tom, of his father's will).

Tom laughed a little, but looked disturbed. His wife had said something to the same effect, and his mother had spoken once or twice in her letters of the prospect of starting the mill again. He was not a bit of a business man, and he did not feel certain, with the theories which he had arrived at of the state of the country, that it was safe yet to spend the money which would have to be spent in putting the mill in order. "They think that the minute it is going again we shall be making money hand over hand, just as father did when we were children," he said. "It is going to cost us no end of money before we can make anything. Before father died he meant to put in a good deal of new machinery, I remember. I don't know anything about the business myself, and I would have sold out long ago if I had an offer that came anywhere near the value. The larger mills are the only ones that are good for anything now, and we should have to bring a crowd of French Canadians here; the day is past for the people who live in this part of the country to go into the factory again. Even the Irish all go West when they come into the country, and don't come to places like this any more."

"But there are a good many of the old work-people down in the village," said Mrs. Wilson. "Jack Towne asked me the other day if you weren't going to start up in the spring."

Tom moved uneasily in his chair, "I'll put you in for superintendent, if you like," he said half angrily, whereupon Mary threw the newspaper at him; but by the time he had thrown it back he was in good humor again.

"Do you know, Tom," she said with amazing seriousness, "That I believe I should like nothing in the world so much as to be the head of a large business? I hate keeping house,—I always did; and I never did so much of it in all my life put together as I have since I have been married. I suppose it isn't womanly to say so, but if I could escape from the whole thing I believe I should be perfectly happy. If you get rich when the mill is going again, I shall beg for a housekeeper, and shirk everything. I give you fair warning. I don't believe I keep this house half so well as you did before I came here."

Tom's eyes twinkled. "I am going to have that glory,—I don't think you do, Polly; but you can't say that I have not been forbearing. I certainly have not told you more than twice how we used to have things cooked. I'm not going to be your kitchen-colonel."

"Of course it seemed the proper thing to do," said his wife, meditatively; "but I think we should have been even happier than we have if I had been spared it. I have had some days of wretchedness that I shudder to think of. I never know what to have for breakfast; and I ought not to say it, but I don't mind the sight of dust. I look upon housekeeping as my life's great discipline," and at this pathetic confession they both laughed heartily.

"I've a great mind to take it off your hands," said Tom. "I always rather liked it, to tell the truth, and I ought to be a better housekeeper,—I have been at it for five years; though housekeeping for one is different from what it is for two, and one of them a woman. You see you have brought a different element into my family. Luckily, the servants are pretty well drilled. I do think you upset them a good deal at first!"

Mary Wilson smiled as if she only half heard what he was saying. She drummed with her foot on the floor and looked intently at the fire, and presently gave it a vigorous poking. "Well?" said Tom, after he had waited patiently as long as he could.

"Tom! I'm going to propose something to you. I wish you would really do as you said, and take all the home affairs under your care, and let me start the mill. I am certain I could manage it. Of course I should get people who understood the thing to teach me. I believe I was made for it; I should like it above all things. And this is what I will do: I will bear the cost of starting it, myself,—I think I have money enough, or can get it; and if I have not put affairs in the right trim at the end of a year I will stop, and you may make some other arrangement. If I have, you and your mother and sister can pay me back."

"So I am going to be the wife, and you the husband," said Tom, a little indignantly; "at least, that is what people will say. It's a regular Darby and Joan affair, and you think you can do more work in a day than I can do in three. Do you know that you must go to town to buy cotton? And do you know there are a thousand things about it that you don't know?"

"And never will?" said Mary, with perfect good humor. "Why, Tom, I can learn as well as you, and a good deal better, for I like business, and you don't. You forget that I was always father's right-hand man after I was a dozen years old, and that you have let me invest my money and some of your own, and I haven't made a blunder yet."

Tom thought that his wife had never looked so handsome or so happy. "I don't care. I should rather like the fun of knowing what people will say. It is a new departure, at any rate. Women think they can do everything better than men in these days, but I'm the first man, apparently, who has wished he were a woman."

"Of course people will laugh," said Mary, "but they will say that it's just like me, and think I am fortunate to have married a man who will let me do as I choose. I don't see why it isn't sensible: you will be living exactly as you were before you married, as to home affairs; and since it was a good thing for you to know something about housekeeping then, I can't imagine why you shouldn't go on with it now, since it makes me miserable, and I am wasting a fine business talent while I do it. What do we care for people's talking about it?"

"It seems to me that it is something like women's smoking: it isn't wicked, but it isn't the custom of the country. And I don't like the idea of your going among business men. Of course I should be above going with you, and having people think I must be an idiot; they would say that you married a manufacturing interest, and I was thrown in. I can foresee that my pride is going to be humbled to the dust in every way," Tom declared in mournful tones, and began to shake with laughter. "It is one of your lovely castles in the air, dear Polly, but an old brick mill needs a better foundation than the clouds. No, I'll look around, and get an honest experienced man for agent. I suppose it's the best thing we can do, for the machinery ought not to lie still any longer; but I mean to sell the factory as soon as I can. I devoutly wish it would take fire, for the insurance would be the best price we are likely to get. That is a famous letter from Alice! I am afraid the captain has been growling over his pay, or they have been giving too many little dinners on board ship. If we were rid of the mill, you and I might go out there this winter. It would be capital fun."

Mary smiled again in an absent-minded way. Tom had an uneasy feeling that he had not heard the end of it yet, but nothing more was said for a day to two. Then Mrs. Tom Wilson announced, with no apparent thought of being contradicted, that she had entirely made up her mind, and she meant to see those men who had been overseers of the different departments, who still lived in the village, and have the mill put in order at once. Tom looked disturbed, but made no opposition; and soon after breakfast his wife formally presented him with a handful of keys, and told him there was some lamb in the house for dinner; and presently he heard the wheels of her little phaeton rattling off down the road. I should be untruthful if I tried to persuade any one that he was not provoked; he thought she would at least have waited for his formal permission, and at first he meant to take another horse, and chase her, and bring her back in disgrace, and put a stop to the whole thing. But something assured him that she knew what she was about, and he determined to let her have her own way. If she failed, it might do no harm, and this was the only ungallant thought he gave her. He was sure that she would do nothing unladylike, or be unmindful of his dignity; and he believed it would be looked upon as one of her odd, independent freaks, which always had won respect in the end, however much they had been laughed at in the beginning. "Susan," said he, as that estimable person went by the door with the dust-pan, "you may tell Catherine to come to me for orders about the house, and you may do so yourself. I am going to take charge again, as I did before I was married. It is no trouble to me, and Mrs. Wilson dislikes it. Besides, she is going into business, and will have a great deal else to think of."

"Yes, sir; very well, sir," said Susan, who was suddenly moved to ask so many questions that she was utterly silent. But her master looked very happy; there was evidently no disapproval of his wife; and she went on up the stairs, and began to sweep them down, knocking the dust-brush about excitedly, as if she were trying to kill a descending colony of insects.

Tom went out to the stable and mounted his horse, which had been waiting for him to take his customary after-breakfast ride to the post-office, and he galloped down the road in quest of the phaeton. He saw Mary talking with Jack Towne, who had been an overseer and a valued workman of his father's. He was looking much surprised and pleased.

"I wasn't caring so much about getting work, myself," he explained; "I've got what will carry me and my wife through; but it'll be better for the young folks about here to work near home. My nephews are wanting something to do; they were going to Lynn next week. I don't say but I should like to be to work in the old place again. I've sort of missed it, since we shut down."

"I'm sorry I was so long in overtaking you," said Tom, politely, to his wife. "Well, Jack, did Mrs. Wilson tell you she's going to start the mill? You must give her all the help you can."

"Deed I will," said Mr. Towne, gallantly, without a bit of astonishment.

"I don't know much about the business yet," said Mrs. Wilson, who had been a little overcome at Jack Towne's lingo of the different rooms and machinery, and who felt an overpowering sense of having a great deal before her in the next few weeks. "By the time the mill is ready, I will be ready, too," she said, taking heart a little; and Tom, who was quick to understand her moods, could not help laughing, as he rode alongside. "We want a new barrel of flour, Tom, dear," she said, by way of punishment for his untimely mirth.

If she lost courage in the long delay, or was disheartened at the steady call for funds, she made no sign; and after a while the mill started up, and her cares were lightened, so that she told Tom that before next pay day she would like to go to Boston for a few days, and go to the theatre, and have a frolic and rest. She really looked pale and thin, and she said she never worked so hard in all her life; but nobody knew how happy she was, and she was glad she had married Tom, for some men would have laughed at it.

"I laughed at it," said Tom meekly. "All is, if I don't cry by and by because I am a beggar, I shall be lucky." But Mary looked fearlessly serene, and said that there was no danger at present.

It would have been ridiculous to expect a dividend the first year, though the Nagasaki people were pacified with difficulty. All the business letters came to Tom's address, and everybody who was not directly concerned thought that he was the motive power of the reawakened enterprise. Sometimes business people came to the mill, and were amazed at having to confer with Mrs. Wilson, but they soon had to respect her talents and her success. She was helped by the old clerk, who had been promptly recalled and reinstated, and she certainly did capitally well. She was laughed at, as she had expected to be, and people said they should think Tom would be ashamed of himself; but it soon appeared that he was not to blame, and what reproach was offered was on the score of his wife's oddity. There was nothing about the mill that she did not understand before very long, and at the end of the second year she declared a small dividend with great pride and triumph. And she was congratulated on her success, and every one thought of her project in a different way from the way they had thought of it in the beginning. She had singularly good fortune: at the end of the third year she was making money for herself and her friends faster than most people were, and approving letters began to come from Nagasaki. The Ashtons had been ordered to stay in that region, and it was evident that they were continually being obliged to entertain more instead of less. Their children were growing fast, too, and constantly becoming more expensive. The captain and his wife had already begun to congratulate themselves secretly that their two sons would in all probability come into possession, one day, of their uncle Tom's handsome property.

For a good while Tom enjoyed life, and went on his quiet way serenely. He was anxious at first, for he thought that Mary was going to make ducks and

drakes of his money and her own. And then he did not exactly like the looks of
the thing, either; he feared that his wife was growing successful as a business
person at the risk of losing her womanliness. But as time went on, and he found
there was no fear of that, he accepted the situation philosophically. He gave up
his collection of engravings, having become more interested in one of coins and
medals, which took up most of his leisure time. He often went to the city in
pursuit of such treasures, and gained much renown in certain quarters as a
numismatologist of great skill and experience. But at last his house (which had
almost kept itself, and had given him little to do beside ordering the dinners,
while faithful old Catherine and her niece Susan were his aids) suddenly became
a great care to him. Catherine, who had been the main-stay of the family for
many years, died after a short illness, and Susan must needs choose that time, of
all others, for being married to one of the second hands in the mill. There
followed a long and dismal season of experimenting, and for a time there was
a procession of incapable creatures going in at one kitchen door and out of the
other. His wife would not have liked to say so, but it seemed to her that Tom
was growing fussy about the house affairs, and took more notice of those minor
details than he used. She wished more than once, when she was tired, that he
would not talk so much about the housekeeping; he seemed sometimes to have
no other thought.

In the early days of Mrs. Wilson's business life, she had made it a rule to
consult her husband on every subject of importance; but it had speedily proved
to be a formality. Tom tried manfully to show a deep interest which he did not
feel, and his wife gave up, little by little, telling him much about her affairs. She
said that she liked to drop business when she came home in the evening; at last
she fell into the habit of taking a nap on the library sofa, while Tom, who could
not use his eyes much by lamp-light, sat smoking or in utter idleness before the
fire. When they were first married his wife had made it a rule that she should
always read him the evening papers, and afterward they had always gone on with
some book of history or philosophy, in which they were both interested. These
evenings of their early married life had been charming to both of them, and from
time to time one would say to the other that they ought to take up again the habit
of reading together. Mary was so unaffectedly tired in the evening that Tom
never liked to propose a walk; for, though he was not a man of peculiarly social
nature, he had always been accustomed to pay an occasional evening visit to his
neighbors in the village. And though he had little interest in the business world,
and still less knowledge of it, after a while he wished that his wife would have
more to say about what she was planning and doing, or how things were getting
on. He thought that her chief aid, old Mr. Jackson, was far more in her thoughts
than he. She was forever quoting Jackson's opinions. He did not like to find that
she took it for granted that he was not interested in the welfare of his own
property; it made him feel like a sort of pensioner and dependent, though when
they had guests at the house, which was by no means seldom, there was nothing

in her manner that would imply that she thought herself in any way the head of the family. It was hard work to find fault with his wife in any way, though, to give him his due, he rarely tried.

But, this being a wholly unnatural state of things, the reader must expect to hear of its change at last, and the first blow from the enemy was dealt by an old woman, who lived nearby, and who called to Tom one morning, as he was driving down to the village in a great hurry (to post a letter, which ordered his agent to secure a long-wished-for ancient copper coin, at any price), to ask him if they had made yeast that week, and if she could borrow a cupful, as her own had met with some misfortune. Tom was instantly in a rage, and he mentally condemned her to some undeserved fate but told her aloud to go and see the cook. This slight delay, besides being killing to his dignity, caused him to lose the mail, and in the end his much desired copper coin. It was a hard day for him, altogether; it was Wednesday and the first days of the week having been stormy the washing was very late. And Mary came home to dinner provokingly good-natured. She had met an old schoolmate and her husband driving home from the mountains and had first taken them over her factory, to their great amusement and delight, and then had brought them home to dinner. Tom greeted them cordially, and manifested his usual graceful hospitality; but the minute he saw his wife alone he said in a plaintive tone of rebuke, "I should think you might have remembered that the servants are unusually busy today. I do wish you would take a little interest in things at home. The women have been washing, and I'm sure I don't know what sort of a dinner we can give your friends. I wish you had thought to bring home some steak. I have been busy myself, and couldn't go down to the village. I thought we would only have a lunch."

Mary was hungry, but she said nothing, except that it would be all right,—she didn't mind; and perhaps they could have some canned soup.

She often went to town to buy or look at cotton, or to see some improvement in machinery, and she brought home beautiful bits of furniture and new pictures for the house, and showed a touching thoughtfulness in remembering Tom's fancies; but somehow he had an uneasy suspicion that she could get along pretty well without him when it came to the deeper wishes and hopes of her life, and that her most important concerns were all matters in which he had no share. He seemed to himself to have merged his life in his wife's; he lost interest in things outside the house and grounds; he felt himself fast growing rusty and behind the times, and to have somehow missed a good deal in life; he had a suspicion that he was a failure. One day the thought rushed over him that his had been almost exactly the experience of most women, and he wondered if it really was any more disappointing and ignominious to him than it was to women themselves. "Some of them may be contented with it," he said to himself, soberly. "People think women are designed for such careers by nature, but I don't know why I ever made such a fool of myself."

Having once seen his situation in life from such a standpoint, he felt it day by day to be more degrading, and he wondered what he should do about it; and once, drawn by a new, strange sympathy, he went to the little family burying-ground. It was one of the mild, dim days that come sometimes in early November, when the pale sunlight is like the pathetic smile of a sad face, and he sat for a long time on the limp, frost-bitten grass beside his mother's grave.

But when he went home in the twilight his step-mother, who just then was making them a little visit, mentioned that she had been looking through some boxes of hers that had been packed long before and stowed away in the garret. "Everything looks very nice up there," she said, in her wheezing voice (which, worse than usual that day, always made him nervous), and added, without any intentional slight to his feelings. "I do think you have always been a most excellent housekeeper."

"I'm tired of such nonsense!" he exclaimed, with surprising indignation. "Mary, I wish you to arrange your affairs so that you can leave them for six months at least. I am going to spend this winter in Europe."

"Why, Tom, dear!" said his wife, appealingly. "I couldn't leave my business any way in the"—

But she caught sight of a look in his usually placid countenance that was something more than decision, and refrained from saying anything more.

And three weeks from that day they sailed.

BY THE NORTH GATE

Joyce Carol Oates

The first time something strange happened to him, the old man, Revere, had felt it descend down upon him like an opaque white mist, something which was still part of his dream and would not let him wake. He had been dreaming of the past again that night, and his dream had been fragmented and confused, like pieces of a jigsaw puzzle spilled across his mind.

He had dreamed first of the winter his wife had died—not of her death, really, but of the house as she lay dying, with her two sisters at her bedside, whispering, and whispering at mealtimes, strangers to him—and he had dreamed of his childhood, oddly so long ago, and of the schoolteacher in the old schoolhouse down the road. These memories had flattened as if they were no more than photographs, and he saw them from a distance, until all the land he owned, and the road, and the jungle-like expanse of the countryside lay before him. It was not the daylight world but another world, and at first he thought it must be his picture of what the land had been like before anyone had come to it. He sometimes thought about things like that—his grandfather had been one of the first settlers here—and Revere, though he could hardly remember the old man, felt a strange kinship with him. But then he saw in his dream that there were already people there: men working in fields, children dawdling to school, and that all of them were surrounded by the great pressure of the forest and of weeds, acres of weeds, pressing in on them. He remembered thinking clearly: I spent sixty-eight years fighting those weeds—sixty-eight years. Then the discomforting scene changed to a fine white mist, and he felt himself rising through it as if through water; rising, soaring to air, to life, having cheated death at least one more day. He knew before he woke that something strange had happened. Maybe in the house, maybe outside. And, later, as he groped around in the near dark—the sun would not rise for another half hour—he heard the hound whining, and his fingers froze to the cold buttons of his shirt. It was Nell. He could hear her in the shed, whining, scratching against the screen door. When he opened the door the dog crawled across the threshold to him, shivering. "Hey, what's wrong with the hound? Too cold for you?" he laughed, but then his laughter stopped. He stooped and saw what was wrong: The dog's ears had been slit, neatly and viciously, and were now crusted with dried blood. Revere held the dog trembling against him, trembling himself, and looked off to the screen door and beyond to the grass blurred with dew, and to his farm buildings and the outer blur of his land, just waking to light.

That had been the day before. Now Revere stood in the shed by his house and stared in bewilderment at his barn. Somehow the sight of the white smoke rising slowly behind the barn and memory of the dog's ears, its anxious eyes, came to him at the same time: He saw them together, and he both realized something and doubted everything.

At first he had thought the barn was on fire, but running out as far as the pump he could see that only the grass in the field behind the barn was burning. The wind came from the northwest, from the mountains far to the north, and gently fanned the flames. Sometimes the narrow fire would die down, and white smoke would rise in a puff; but in the next instant the flames would reappear, slyly, slanting up over the top of the grass, bent flat by the wind. Revere grabbed both wooden buckets and filled them at the pump; then he set them down and ran back to the shed, muttering to himself, and got a broom that was propped up in a corner with a fine network of cobwebs about it. Running back again, he thought; I ought to of fired that field myself. But I guess I would of done it when there wasn't all that wind.

Behind the barn the fire inched away from him. The field seemed to be dissolving in white smoke; and sometimes hidden from him, sometimes piercing to his eyes, toothlike flames flared upward. Far to the right the hay barn tilted, looking as if it were leaning away in fear. Revere stared at it as he stumbled across the field. "It ain't gettin' to you," he muttered. He began beating wildly at the flames with the broom, now and then looking around at the hay barn. It was still safe. He worked for some time. "Least I'll get this field cleaned," he thought, but he could not fool himself with such thoughts for long; as he stood with his heels in the dirt, slamming at the flames, his breath searing his throat, he knew that he could not fool himself. Nothing he might think up later, nothing he could contrive into words, would make up for what he must endure now. The air had turned to shimmering heat, the broom was smoldering, and there was a black burnt spot on his trousers that he thought might be widening; but it was all right. The fire was nearly out now, and he was all right—there was only a patch of it left, small flames licking at the dry tufts of grass near the ground. He poured water on it. The milky smoke curled up. He was turning, the creaking bucket in his hand, when something happened. A great wave of heat struck him, conspiring with the weariness inside his head; something slammed against his back and he lay still.

He woke at about noon. He was lying on his back where he had fallen. He got stiffly to his feet, blinking in confusion and shame, and when he looked at the field he was astonished at how small the fire had been. It had come nowhere near the hay barn or even the fence on the other side. He stared at it almost as if he were disappointed. In that moment the world shimmered about him, hot and opaque and gently mocking. He could not remember falling; he could not think how it had happened. But when he felt the familiar weariness in his back and legs he understood; he understood why he had fallen there and why he had fallen the other time—on the road coming from the store when some children had been running after him and throwing pieces of dried mud, shouting, "Old Revere! Old man Revere!"

He looked around at his land. The summer sky looked hardened by heat, and beneath it the land lay still, save for where the wind prodded it—fluttering of leaves and slow, graceful eclipsing of light by shadow. When he turned back, the hound, Nell, rose from where she had been lying and ran to him. "Yes, it's all right," he said, stroking the dog's head. He looked around as if he thought someone might be watching. "Don't you worry about me. I'm feelin' better now." He went back to the house.

Now he sat on the bench by the shed door and rested in the sunlight, looking at the barn and thinking about the smoke and the dog's ears. Around the corner blackbirds were rioting in the cherry tree, but he did not have the strength to get up to chase them away. Not that it mattered, for he had given up picking the cherries long ago, and besides they were small and often wormy. Thinking of cherries ought to have made him hungry and he felt a vague dutiful notion to go in and eat; but he did not move. Overhead the sun moved past the peak of the house, and the shadow in which he sat extended to his feet. The dog lay before him, sleeping, and sometimes stretched out her legs as if she were pushing something away.

Revere watched the hound and thought about what had happened. He knew that something had happened. And there had to be a reason for it—a reason he must try to discover. He had always had faith in understanding and knowledge, the kind of thinking found in books, though Heaven knew he had never been good at it himself. He had never read a word until he was thirty, and only then when the schoolteacher had taken such pains with him, acting serious all the time, refusing to give in and laugh at a grown man doing a child's lessons. Revere felt a sudden flash of warmth for the man; he had liked him fine. But after so long, after such work, he had forgotten everything; he found one day, when he tried to read again, that it had slipped away from him. He was as ashamed of that now, thirty-eight years later, as he had been on that day. So much time wasted. He used to go over to the schoolhouse after the children left, every afternoon, and the schoolteacher—a young man afraid of the big boys—would talk to him and show him books, books he would like Revere to read later on, books with colored binding, with gold letters in a glass case at the front of the room. Chalk dust would hang in the silent air. When Revere spoke it would be slowly and politely, not the way he bawled orders at home. He could never understand why the young man did not laugh at him. He wanted to learn; he felt the young man's strange desire to teach him; but when it was time to speak or read—why, Revere would stare at the print and at his big thumbs on either page, and everything would get mixed up. Revere, filled with shame, could not look up at the teacher.

One winter there was trouble: A boy had struck the teacher; he had fallen. Revere never found out how seriously he was hurt, or what happened to him after he left. The schoolhouse was boarded up for a while, then opened again a few years later, for the winter months. But now it was closed again and had been closed for about three years. If children wanted to go to school, they had to go somewhere else, miles away. On his walks Revere often crossed the fields to the school, and there he would sit on the stone steps and think. His feet would sprawl idly before him. The old building was in disrepair, its windows boarded up crazily, and looking at it made Revere feel bad. He would sit and think of the past and of the school on those dark winter afternoons, of the young man's careful, friendly voice. . . . The schoolhouse was the key to one of his secrets. It was there that his saddest failure had occurred; but that failure was not really something he wanted to forget. As if he felt the necessity to remember, he would return again and again to the ruined school and, sitting on the steps, stare dreamily out at the wild grass and the dirt road and the field beyond. Sometimes a farmer would be in the field working a team, and he would come to the fence and lean over, settling himself for a talk. Revere always felt that he must know the man, but at that distance he could not be sure—his eyes were not so good any more—and he had to smile and nod as if he understood everything well.

"You, Revere," the man would say. His face was broad and tanned, and snatches of yellow hair showed beneath his straw hat. "Ain't you got nothin' to do at home? Ain't there somethin' there you should see to?"

Revere supposed this was a joke, so he would laugh an old man's cackle and answer, "It goes on by itself."

"Is that so?" the man would say, spitting toward the ditch. "You sure of that now?"

"Always was like that," Revere would say. He felt both cheerful and discomforted, but he would laugh just the same, as if the man's words struck him as funny.

"You watch out life don't catch up with you," the farmer would say.

"I stood it sixty-eight years now," Revere would answer.

After a while the man's eyes would move away and he would gradually seem to forget Revere, as if the old man did not matter. His hands would be busy pulling absently and viciously at stalks of grass growing by the fence posts, pulling them out and shredding them in his strong fingers, and letting the wind blow the pieces away.

When Revere went home the sight of the farm always discouraged him; he could not believe it had fallen into such disrepair. The barns looked tilted—they did for a fact—and the yard was wild with grass gone to seed, and chickens running loose that did not know him, and pieces of wire and stones and old wheels lying around: chicken fencing, boards, sheets of asbestos, things for which there were no longer any names, all lying around, telling lazily of failure. He would go around them to the house. This at least looked better, though Heaven knew it would never be the same as it had been when his wife was alive and there were the children—the two boys and Nancy, his daughter. It seemed to have changed as if by magic—the shed and the house and the whole look of the land—as soon as he was finally left alone.

Now he stirred on the bench. The dog woke at once. One of her ears had fallen back, showing the pink, scarred inside. As Revere looked at the dog he realized slowly, and with the sense of approaching revelation of sorts, that he was very tired, deathly tired. Only a few years ago he and the boys used to fire the fields, the one behind the barn and the long one by the creek, and then he had been able to work all morning and afternoon and feel nothing except hunger; maybe a little weariness, but mostly hunger. How the boys worked with him, shouting and running with brooms! They had not even worn shirts. . . . But that must have been more than only a few years ago, he thought. His boys Frank and Will, with the blackened brooms over their shoulders, big strong boys, taller than he already, with their dirty faces slit by grins, cuffing each other when he wasn't looking, arguing even at the supper table with their faces washed and their big feet sticking out from under the table. . . . Was it possible that he was their father, that he had made possible their lives, their strength, their fierce awkward affection for him? Later Frank had got into trouble with that knife he had been so proud of buying. The boy he had fought with had died; people said he just lay down and bled as if there was no end to it, and Frank had run, run off on foot, and Revere had never heard from him again. Sometimes his wife would forget that and talk about Frank as if he were still home, and when she lay in her final sickness she often spoke of him, whining that he hadn't come to kiss her good-bye, and her going on such a long journey (though he had never kissed her when he was home; they never did such things). Revere had waited for a few years before he began to think of Frank as dead.

When Will left home he wrote letters back, he wrote five or six of them; and Revere still had them somewhere around the house. In his last letter he said he was traveling somewhere west, to find work with a lot of other men; but they had heard no more from him. Revere remembered Will as the slighter of the two boys, the dark one, the one he had never really gotten to know, and then it was too late. The history of the boy's life with them seemed a mystery, as if a stranger had lived with them, and Revere too stupid to find out much about him. . . . When Frank had run off, it was Will who told him. They had stood outside, right by the shed, and Will's face was wet and his dark hair looked wild and comic. "Frank tole me to tell you he got in some trouble." Will had said. "He—he got in some trouble back there. . . ." The boy's eyes got big and wet, and Revere had been astonished and ready to tell him that boys never cried—until he heard the news. Behind Will one of the big lilac trees was moving a little in the wind, all its flowers shriveled and brown, and around it some chickens were picking in their brisk, alert, ridiculous way, jerking their heads up now and then as if someone had called to them.

Then in Revere's daydream the time changed, and it was later: a wintertime, inside the house. Revere tried to remember which time this was, and why his daughter Nancy was standing by the big bedroom door, and why she looked so stupidly at him. Then he remembered that his wife was sick and that her sisters were in the room, and they must have said something to Nancy; she had run out with her face tightened in anger. "Now you don't pay any attention to them," he had told her, "they're just old—". The Nancy of that day had been married just the summer before and lived with her husband and his folks; she seemed suddenly a stranger; she looked at him as though he were a stranger.

"Oh, and you too! I'm sick of you all!" she had cried. Then she stopped and looked funny and ran to him and took both his hands. "Oh, Pa," she said. Revere's face ached as if it wanted to smile or something, but when he opened his mouth to talk he had nothing to say. He remembered having lifted Nancy high into the air when she was a baby, and swinging her around while the boys shouted and stamped in excitement and his wife pleaded with him to stop; but the memory was only his, not Nancy's; they did not share it; she cared nothing for it. As she held his hands, looking at him he was about to smile but somehow never did. . . .

Then the time changed again, and it was later still—another incident. This time Nancy was talking to him as if it were she and not he who was older. Nancy wanted him to come to live with them in Pools Brook—that was it—but he couldn't quite keep his mind still enough to think about it; he couldn't quite understand it. "I never expected to be eaten up by things, one after the other," he had said to them. Nancy's husband was both embarrassed and impatient; he must have hated to talk to the old man like this, to argue with him about something so trivial. "I wouldn't know how to start over again in another house," he had said. His words had made sense to him, but Nancy had gone on with something different as if she had not even been listening. After a while she had left, angry, and her husband with her; Revere remembered staring after the man, watching them out of his kitchen window. The young man had light hair and small nervous eyes; he too was a stranger, and he and Nancy, walking fast alongside each other but not touching, seemed to be strangers to each other as well. Revere felt a pang of guilt, as if he had betrayed Nancy, as he had betrayed his sons, by bringing them into a world of strangers. There was something perplexing about it, but it was too difficult for him to think of and made him feel bad, and already his mind was confused with other things.

Like hungry flies, his thoughts buzzed around inside his head. Now it was an old unfinished argument with the schoolteacher he was thinking of, and now his wife; now, a handsaw someone had borrowed and never returned; now, his wife's sisters jealously guarding her death amid a smell of moth balls, with the curtains moving in that spring's late, sickly light. . . .

Then Revere woke with a start. His heart pounded furiously. He was slouched on the bench, but he straightened and stared about the cluttered yard as if ready to jump up and challenge anyone who was there. The yard was empty. Behind the barn the field was blurred. He rubbed his eyes, but he could see no better; green grass and burnt grass melted into one another. He looked at things closer to him, safer to look at. Nell had gone, and the grass was still flattened where she had been lying. "Well," he said, yawning, "I s'pose I am gettin' old, to need sleep like that after such a little fire. . . . Only a little fire. . . ." He mumbled to himself without listening. He was going to stand, and his legs were tensed for the effort; but for some reason he did not stand. He remained on the bench, his head bowed, his eyes on the dust at his feet. There was something he must think of, something he must understand; but he was not sure just what it was. At last he stood up and went inside the house. There he listened for the dog, for the sound of her toenails on the rough planking of the shed. After a while, as he put together something to eat, moving wearily from place to place, grunting aloud, he forgot what he had been listening for.

When Revere had finished the meal, he stayed seated at the old table, his arms out before him, staring at the window with its blind, dull orange glow. Then he happened to look around and saw someone standing at the door. He only happened to look around; he had not heard any sound. A young boy stood peering through the loose screen of the door. For a moment Revere and the boy stared at each other. Then the boy said, "Mister, could you come out here a minute?"

Revere was angry that his heart was pounding so. He got up and went to the door. "What do you want?" he said. He and the boy glanced toward the shed doorway, as if both knew there was someone else out there. The boy was smiling a broad, peculiar way. "Somebody to see me? Your pa, maybe?" Revere asked. But he did not know who the boy was. There were so many young people around, boys growing up, nearly men, he could no longer keep track of them all. "Your pa out there?" he said.

"Ain't my pa," said the boy. He came up to about Revere's chin—a heavy, strong boy, about twelve, with a tanned face and dirty blond hair. He went ahead of Revere.

Outside stood two other boys. Revere shaded his eyes. "Anything I can do for you?" he said. He supposed he knew their fathers or grandfathers, but no name came to mind. The tallest of the three stood with a grimy bare foot on Revere's bench. He had almost white hair and pale eyebrows and eyelashes; he was smiling at Revere. "You want to fish off my land?" Revere said, though he saw before the words were out that they carried no poles. "You can take that path there—".

"Ain't fish we're interested in today," the tall boy said. "We wondered if we could. . . " He looked at Revere evenly, while the other two smiled identically and gazed up past Revere's head to the roof of the house. "We wondered if we could use some of your water there."

"You never needed to ask," said Revere.

He waved toward the pump. But the boys did not move, and the tallest one leaned over the bench and spat into the dust as if he was tired of waiting for something. The heavy one—the one who had come to Revere's door, the one with the careful blank face and a round stomach, prominent under his overalls—simply watched. And the third boy, the youngest, stood with his two upper front teeth catching his lower lip in a precarious, tickled smile. "It's right there. You go ahead," said Revere. Running to the pump, the two bigger boys poked at the other, not looking back at Revere. He watched as the fat boy took hold of the pump handle as if testing it and began pumping. Water splashed down onto the wooden planks. Revere waited, and he saw with a strange, weakening sense of dismay—a sense of something within him dissolving, collapsing—that they had no bottles or buckets, that they simply stood around the glistening platform while the fat boy pumped, the old pump handle creaking, the water splashing down onto the planks. The fat boy was jerking the pump handle up as high as it would go, even jumping a little with it, looking so funny that the other two laughed—the little boy especially, laughing with his eyes pinched blind, his hands slapping at his thighs like a grown man's. After about five minutes they lost interest.

They whispered together and looked back at Revere. Revere was conscious of himself: an old man standing before his rotting house, his thin white hair wild about his head, his arms raised in an absurd gesture of alarm. The boys jumped off the pump platform and started back. The fat one came first. He was smiling now, and as he neared Revere the old man could see drops of water on his face, as though the boy had been out in the rain. "My brothers an' me want to thank you kindly," he said. The other boys laughed. The fat boy did not glance at them but wiped his forehead importantly. The back of his hand, suddenly uplifted, was smeared with dirt and something red, maybe paint. Revere did not know what to say. "We were all hot before," the fat boy said chattily.

"We been walkin'," the little boy said.

"Yes," said the fat boy. "That will fix us up fine."

Revere waited. There seemed to be something they expected of him. "I don't understand," he said.

"Well you got them-there white whiskers," the fat boy said. The others laughed, and the fat boy laughed too, suddenly, as if he hadn't meant to but couldn't help it. He looked past Revere, up to the roof of the house or to the sky. "Well, I guess we'll be goin' now."

"We got to eat supper," the little boy said.

"We can't stay," the fat boy said. "I guess we'll be back though. We'll be back tomorrow."

They turned and went back along the path. Revere watched them. He watched them with a dull pain beginning in his chest, maybe in his heart. By the pump the boys looked around. "You got yourself some flies there," the fat boy called in a high, singsong voice.

"What?" said Revere. "What?"

"Some flies there." The boys laughed together, their faces blurred across the distance. "Lots of flies around the corner there." They turned and ran. Revere stood with his heart pounding madly as before. Then he went to the corner of the shed. The ground was barren and stony there and had eroded sharply away from the house. A few feet away stood the lilac tree that had always been stunted, stunted in the shade of the house. . . . Revere stopped suddenly. He was about to call to the dog, when he noticed the deep gash in her stomach, and the blood, and the glinting circle of flies buzzing around her. He ran, sliding on the rocky ground, to her side. As he bent over, flies grazed his face. He touched the dog's head; her eyes were open and wet and seemed to be looking at him.

He got up, scrambling, knocking pebbles downhill, and went back to the corner of the house. His eyes had turned so weak, it did not seem possible they could betray him like this when he needed them so desperately. He stumbled on down the path. He thought of what he would say to the boys when he found them, how he would shout, how sternly, with what furious strength he would confront them, how they would cringe—they were only boys! But when he began shouting hoarsely, "You there! You boys! Come back here . . ." he felt he did not know what else to say. He was hurrying, stumbling. He could not always see the ground; it seemed to jerk beneath him. He stopped by a rusty overturned barrel to catch his breath.

How weak his eyes had become! Revere knew what his land and barns looked like, so he could fill in details that were now blurred and gone; but he could not really see them. Or the grass either. It was made of millions of little stalks, moving in the wind, but to Revere it looked like a solid green river. The boys were gone. "Why did you do that?" he cried. He shook his fist. "Why did you? Why did you come on my land to do that?" A skinny white chicken darted away, clucking in terror. "You tell me why you did it!" Revere shouted. "I never done nothin' to any man, not a one of them, I never got born to fight. . . ." He stared in anger at his own trembling hands. The sunlight was quiet about him but—try though he did—he could not see the boys anywhere, not hiding in the grass or looking at him around the corner of his barn. He thought of the children running after him on the road that day, and how he had joked with them at first and then had seen that they were not laughing with him, but only staring at him, their little hands raised and about to throw something at him. "You old Revere!" they had cried, but it was not because he was a Revere, not because he was who he was—there was no reason for their behavior. Now he stared at the fine golden glow that had begun to descend upon the countryside, on the tops of the waving blades of grass, imparting a strange soft light to his own familiar land, as if an answer to his questions might somehow come from out of nowhere. To the wavering abstract pictures of the boys that remained in his memory, he shouted, "You come back! Come back here! All my life I done battle against it: that life don't mean nothin'! That it don't make sense! Sixty-eight years of battle, so you come back! You listen to me! You ain't goin' to change my mind now, an' me grown so old an' come so far. . . ."

The wind eased upon him from the northwest again. It touched his tearful squinting eyes and his raised fist. "All of sixty-eight years," he said, this time to

himself, with the air of one telling a secret. "Sixty-eight years I fought it . . . an'
I never give in, not once. Not with Frank even. . . . I never give in." He
believed there was something he should do, something a man ought to do, even
an old man; but it would never get to the beginning of things. It would never get
through. At the rim of his consciousness the faces of the boys floated, but they
no longer possessed any identity, any individuality. By an effort of the will that
exhausted him, that strained his mind and even his heart, he saw them enveloped
by a greater darkness beyond them, the darkness of this wild land itself; he saw
them caught within the accidental pattern of a fate in which he himself would be
caught. "But they ain't no judgment upon the world," he said scornfully. "They
ain't anything but boys, no more. No more than that. They don't stand for
anything s'post to change my mind about life."

His thoughts built up and collapsed about him. He stood on the path and stared
at his blackened shoes while his hand groped along the side of the rusted barrel,
coming away flaked with soft rust. He sat down heavily. The barrel rolled a little
forward and stopped, then rolled back to its groove in the earth; and Revere sat
with his feet out before him, his legs stiff and tensed and weak all at once. "This
here ain't no more than a accident," he mumbled, and then to his slow delight
everything seemed clear. He felt he was arguing with the young man who had
taught school down the road so long ago. It was in such a way they had argued,
argued about life, about strange things—no one else had ever talked to Revere
like that, not even his wife, not even his father—and Revere would give his side
and, knowing all along he was right, would leave out parts so that the teacher
could fill them in. What had they talked about—with the schoolroom warm and
dusty around them, emptied of the children, and the windows already showing
dark at five-thirty, and the schoolteacher with his worried eyes, his abstract gaze,
who thought so long before he spoke—what was it they had talked about?

One time, one winter afternoon, they had talked about stories, in particular
about a story Revere had just finished reading (it had taken him about a week to
do so, trying to figure out the words before the teacher told him what they were,
reading painfully aloud). The story was about magic and things happening in a
past time, in another world; it was about a young girl, and death and disorder
that befell her, that came to her in the form of a dark man. "It don't make no
sense," Revere had said, pretending more scorn than he felt and looking slyly up
at the teacher, "cause things don't happen that way in the world." The teacher
had had an answer, but Revere could not remember it. He did remember that
time, though, and the smell of chalk and dust and the coal burning in the stove
at his back, and it seemed good to remember just the same, good to remember.
All the strange failures of his life, all its picking torment, even this final
vexatious waiting for death—all shrank before his memory of that time, the way
his childhood nightmares had shrunk back, vanquished, before the clear empty
sunshine of the day.

PART TWO

NEW ADAMS UNDERGOING TRANSFORMATION

In contrast to the men in Part One, the New Adams in this section seem to struggle into states of greater happiness—or at least the possibility of it. None of them is completely joyful at the end of their stories, but all seem more able to experience and to give more joy as a result of their painful transformations.

Pain and a "reawakened" "driving want for human sympathy and companionship" are what propel Kate Chopin's M'sieur Michel through his transformation in "After the Winter." Self-exiled to "a kennel of a cabin on the hill" where he curses men and God after the loss, twenty-five years ago, of his young wife and child, Michel is lonely and miserable. He is on the verge of surrendering to a feeling as "bitter as hate" when a young Acadian girl and her two childlike companions take the flowers from around his hut for Easter church decorations while he is away. Enraged by this "violation" of his solitude, Michel hastens down the hill to the church, where the joyful "mysterious hidden quality" of the Easter music sends him in a panicked retreat to his hut—and to a state of "unbounded restlessness." In this state, in which a "longing had sprung up within him as sharp as pain and not to be appeased," Michel finds himself walking through the moonlight to the "bit of land" he had farmed and lived on happily with his wife and child. Enraptured by the beauty of his Edenic "smooth, green meadow, with cattle huddled upon the cool sward," which has been lovingly cared for and used by his friend Joe Duplan, Michel finally lets go of his inner turmoil at the urging of Duplan. At the end of the story, we see this Acadian New Adam emerging from his emotional "winter" and holding out his arms to reconnect with his friend, with the "radiant" land, and with "an infinite peace that seemed to descend upon him and envelop him."

Even more in communion with Nature, Granville Ivanhoe Jordan in June Jordan's poem pores over seed catalogs in his kitchen and saves for money orders so he can "plant the Brooklyn backyard" with "pear and/apple trees/or peaches/in first bloom." "Forced to leave" his beautiful island home, this rather innocent "West Indian in kitchen exile" strikes his daughter as striving unsuccessfully to recreate a somewhat Edenic garden of West Indian life in a city that despises "the sweet calypso/of your trust." Although forced to live in this bleak new world of Brooklyn, this New Adam seems to thwart, through his hope, love, and determination, the ugly forces that would destroy him; his burial ceremony in the West Indies is "lit by sun that cannot be undone/by death." Such transcendence, however limited, holds within itself the seeds of transformation that the New World so desperately needs.

Similarly transcending is the father in Judith Ortiz Cofer's poem. "Stiff and immaculate" in his white Navy uniform, this loving New Adam emerges "from the bellies of iron whales," where he makes sure his ship "parted the waters/on a straight course." "Like the evening prayer," he keeps returning, whenever he can obtain a leave, to his wife, son, and daughter, appearing in his "flash of white . . . like an angel/heralding a new day." His commitment to his family and concern for them bring much joy to him and to his family.

Joe Banks in Zora Neale Hurston's "The Gilded Six Bits" rises above a most painful experience to make a similar commitment to his family and a joyful family life. "It was a Negro yard around a Negro house in a Negro settlement" begins Hurston's story. Into his "happy yard" strides joyful Joe Banks to play a merry payday game in the yard and the little house with his delighted wife, Missie May. Joe is a big, tall, energetic man deeply in love with his young wife. "God took pattern after a pine tree and built you noble," exclaims his equally enamored wife to him. In addition, Hurston tells us that Joe takes pride in his work as a menial laborer. All told, Joe and Missie May are blissfully happy in their country setting by the lake where each dawn "the challenging sun flung a flaming sword from east to west across the trembling water." Alluding thus to the "flaming sword" that God places east of the Garden of Eden in the second Creation account (Genesis 3:24) to guard the tree that gives eternal life, Hurston reminds us that American Adams cannot live in blissful innocence forever. Banks tends to be somewhat possessive of his wife and takes her out to parade her in the new ice cream parlor so that Slemmons, the slick new man in town, can see she is "his woman." When Joe discovers his wife in bed with Slemmons, he does not divorce Missie May or even cover up his hurt, but rather distances himself from her to sort out his confused feelings and to grieve. When Missie May gives birth to a son some months after her adultery, Joe struggles further and then finally decides to accept his wife as flawed. Generously forgiving her, and publicly proclaiming the child as his, Joe joyfully returns to his "happy yard" and his previously playful life with her. While Hurston's readers can perhaps envision a richer life for Joe—particularly in a less racist society—he has clearly experienced a rewarding transformation that involves forging close bonds with his less than perfect Eve and the new child.

Unlike Joe Banks, swaggering O.E. Parker in Flannery O'Connor's gently humorous and symbolical story "Parker's Back" does not feel that he loves his wife at the beginning of their marriage. After living a lonely, restless life in which he drifted from one job to another and got tattooed whenever he felt dissatisfied, Parker seeks out the country and, while selling apples, stumbles upon Sarah Ann, a fundamentalist preacher's daughter. Although she is physically gaunt and rigidly religious and he swears he will never see her again after she refuses to have sex with him, Parker marries her and settles down to a demanding job as a farmhand. He stays with Sarah Ann "as if she had him conjured," though he believes he can figure her out. "It was himself," O'Connor tells us, "he could not understand." He has in fact not even acknowledged his own name, Obadiah.

Parker and his wife live in a house in the country on a "high embankment" which sits alone "save for a single tall pecan tree." One day he hits a tree and is thrown from his tractor, which bursts into flames, incinerating his shoes. Terrified, the barefoot Parker takes off for town where he visits a tattoo artist. Because he could not see his own back, Parker had never bothered to get a tattoo there, but now he spends two days painfully getting his back tattooed with a special present to his wife—a picture of a Byzantine Christ "with all-demanding eyes." Happily anticipating his wife's delight, the next night he returns to Sarah Ann who has not known where he has been. When she refuses to let him in until he identifies himself by his real name, he whispers "Obadiah" and "all at once," Parker says, "he felt the light pouring through him, turning his spider web soul into a perfect arabesque of colors, a garden of trees and birds and beasts." Outraged by his unexplained absence and "blasphemous" tattoo, the pregnant Sarah Ann beats his back with a broom, raising welts on the face of Christ. Deeply hurt, Parker collapses outside under the pecan tree and cries, O'Connor says, "like a baby."

Although Parker has not succeeded in pleasing his wife whom he now knows he loves, he has changed somewhat for the better. He's acknowledged he has no control over such things as tractor accidents and falling in love, he has connected with his feelings for his wife and realized he yearns for family life, and he is trying to reach out, not only to his wife, but also to his God. O'Connor's deliberate identification of Parker with the battered Christ suggests that while he may have a long way to go before he experiences true happiness (he may, for instance, need a more understanding partner than Sarah Ann), he has groped his way into an orientation much more likely to bring him happiness than his previous life as a selfish drifter. This New Adam can journey toward Eden only through this kind of inner transformation of "his spider web soul" into "a garden of trees and birds and beasts."

Toni Cade Bambara's Cliff Hemphill also painfully journeys to a state of greater unselfishness. In Bambara's story "A Tender Man," Cliff is struggling to connect with Aisha, a caring young African-American woman who forthrightly tells him she is "very attracted" to him as one of the "good guys" on campus. Equally forthrightly, Aisha confronts Cliff with the fact that he is not parenting the daughter he had with his former wife, a white woman. Realizing how silly are the "endless control games he liked to play with assertive types," Cliff gropes not only to come to terms with his failures as a father, but also to initiate the "inventory of his self, his life" he feels he has too long postponed. As Cliff begins mentally devising ways to care for his daughter, Aisha asks what he wanted to be when he grew up. Remembering how much he did not want to imitate the father who abandoned him, he replies "a tender man."

Jung might say that Joe Banks, O.E. Parker, and Cliff Hemphill are discovering and nurturing their animas—their inner female principles—when they begin to develop the more tender, loving sides of their natures. Indeed, the concept of the anima seems to very much inform Patricia Goedicke's poem "When He's at His Most Brawling." A man who does not acknowledge his anima, Goedicke seems to be saying, is giving it immense power over him and is experiencing but a fraction of the healing he might otherwise undergo. Says Goedicke:

> When he's at his most brawling
> She's at her most brutally gentle
> And all over him like a silk tent
> Her shimmering laughter
> Like iridescent ice-crystals
> Shatters the high notes
> Of his dark hysteria.

Terrified to the point of hysteria, the man mightily combats here the lure of woman's reality. However, he experiences it as something located deep within him, embodied in a persona so assured of its own worth, so secure in its central place in his reality, so sure of her power, so joyful, and—perhaps—so able to drolly contemplate his absurdly self-imposed misery that she "brutally" abandons herself to her most irresistible gentleness and to joyous laughter, which dissipates at least the higher ranges of his terror.

This clear-eyed image acknowledging not only women's power over men, but also the nature, source, and consequences of that power is but one of many such statements in women's literature that reveal, I think, an unflinching insistence on telling the truth about men and their relationship to women. After all, many of these gifted women writers chafed fiercely at the restraints imposed on them and the privileges denied them by a male-dominated society, and how often do oppressed people anywhere reveal what power they may secretly have over their oppressors? Better to keep it quiet is the way most oppressed people think about any power they may have, lest the oppressors become aware of it and take that modicum of power away, too. But many gifted women seem to have been more interested in getting the truth told, judging not only by these candid portraits of female power, but also by the memorable flaws of such female characters as Missie May and Sarah Ann.

Maybe these fiercely honest, detailed portraits of women's power over men represent a heroic effort by women to try and help people "get at" and understand the underlying twists and turns that have led to the mess of patriarchal society, with its neurotic dependencies and skewed relationships. A man who derives his happiness from his love for a woman is better off, these portraits seem to say, than a man who selfishly and stoically refuses to love anyone besides himself, but, ultimately, this is not the most helpful path to happiness—for either men or women. Certainly that seems to be one purpose of the haunting, compassionately comical story by Carson McCullers entitled "A Tree, a Rock, a Cloud."

In "A Tree, a Rock, a Cloud," a paperboy of twelve is stopped by a man of about sixty as he is leaving a streetcar cafe early one morning. The old man grasps the boy's chin and, turning his face slowly from side to side, says, "I love you." The patrons of the cafe—all men—laugh, and the old man invites the young boy to have a beer with him while he explains. He shows the paperboy some blurred, unflattering pictures of his wife, who left him eleven years ago after living with him for "'one year, nine months, three days, and two nights.'" Stating that love to him is a "science," the old man sadly, gravely—and none too clearly—"explains": "I am a person who feels many things. All my life one thing after another has impressed me. Moonlight. The leg of a pretty girl. . . . But the point is that when I had enjoyed anything there was a peculiar sensation as though it was laying around loose in me. Nothing seemed to finish itself up or fit in with the other things . . . I was a man who had never loved." When he met this woman, he tells the boy solemnly, "There were these beautiful feelings and loose little pleasures inside me. And this woman was something like an assembly line for my soul. I ran these little pieces of myself through her and I come out complete."

After searching for her throughout the Midwest and the South for two years, the old man reports that "around the third year a curious thing began to happen to me." Unable to deliberately call to mind her face anymore, he is suddenly struck at odd moments by an overpowering memory of her that "corners around sideways," instead of hitting him directly, and indicates to him that she had begun to "chase me around in my very soul." His reaction to this turn of events—the experience of being overtaken, which so many women see as terrifying to men—is to fling himself into any sin that suddenly appeals to him for the next two years. In the fifth year, after "she and I had fleed around from each other for so long that finally we just got tangled up together and lay down and quiet," "peace" and his "science" come to him in Portland.

Telling the child to "listen carefully," the old man explains that he "meditated on love and reasoned it out" and "realized what is wrong" with men. What is wrong is that when they fall in love for the first time, they fall in love with "'a woman, . . . without science, with nothing to go by, they undertake the most dangerous and sacred experience in God's earth. . . . They begin at the climax.

. . . Son, do you know how love should be begun?' . . . The old man leaned closer and whispered 'A tree. A rock. A cloud.'"

The man, with an "earnest and bright and wild" face, goes on to detail how he started loving things he would pick up on the street, graduated to a goldfish, and worked his way up to "a street full of people," "a bird in the sky," and then "a traveler on the road," cautiously reserving love for a woman as the "last step in my science." To seal indelibly on our hearts this piercing portrait of a man painfully struggling to learn women's values and to dramatize his female creator's conviction that the power that accrues to women as the source of meaning in so many men's lives needs to be done away with, McCullers ends "A Tree, a Rock, a Cloud" with the boy's statement upon the old man's departure, "He sure has done a lot of traveling."

AFTER THE WINTER

Kate Chopin

I.

Trezinie, the blacksmith's daughter, stepped out upon the gallery just as M'sieur Michel passed by. He did not notice the girl but walked straight on down the village street.

His seven hounds skulked, as usual, about him. At his side hung his powder-horn, and on his shoulder a gunny-bag slackly filled with game that he carried to the store. A broad felt hat shaded his bearded face and in his hand he carelessly swung his old-fashioned rifle. It was doubtless the same with which he had slain so many people, Trezinie shudderingly reflected. For Cami, the cobbler's son—who must have known—had often related to her how this man had killed two Choctaws, as many Texans, a free mulatto and numberless blacks, in that vague locality known as "the hills."

Older people who knew better took little trouble to correct this ghastly record that a younger generation had scored against him. They themselves had come to half-believe that M'sieur Michel might be capable of anything, living as he had, for so many years, apart from humanity, alone with his hounds in a kennel of a cabin on the hill. The time seemed to most of them fainter than a memory when, a lusty young fellow of twenty-five, he had cultivated his strip of land across the lane from Les Cheniers; when home and toil and wife and child were so many benedictions that he humbly thanked heaven for having given him.

But in the early '60's he went with his friend Duplan and the rest of the "Louisiana Tigers." He came back with some of them. He came to find—well, death may lurk in a peaceful valley lying in wait to ensnare the toddling feet of little ones. Then, there are women—there are wives with thoughts that roam and grow wanton with roaming; women whose pulses are stirred by strange voices and eyes that woo; women who forget the claims of yesterday, the hopes of to-morrow, in the impetuous clutch of to-day.

But that was no reason, some people thought, why he should have cursed men who found their blessings where they had left them—cursed God, who had abandoned him.

Persons who met him upon the road had long ago stopped greeting him. What was the use? He never answered them; he spoke to no one; he never so much as looked into men's faces. When he bartered his game and fish at the village store for powder and shot and such scant food as he needed, he did so with few words and less courtesy. Yet feeble as it was, this was the only link that held him to his fellow-beings.

Strange to say, the sight of M'sieur Michel, though more forbidding than ever that delightful spring afternoon, was so suggestive to Trezinie as to be almost an inspiration.

It was Easter eve and the early part of April. The whole earth seemed teeming with new, green, vigorous life everywhere—except the arid spot that immediately surrounded Trezinie. It was no use; she had tried. Nothing would grow among those cinders that filled the yard; in that atmosphere of smoke and flame that was constantly belching from the forge where her father worked at his trade. There were wagon wheels, bolts and bars of iron, plowshares and all manner of unpleasant-looking things littering the bleak, black yard; nothing green anywhere except a few weeds that would force themselves into fence corners. And Trezinie knew that flowers belong to Easter time, just as dyed eggs do. She had plenty of eggs; no one had more or prettier ones; she was not going to grumble about that. But she did feel distressed because she had not a flower to help deck the altar on Easter morning. And every one else seemed to have them in such abundance! There was 'Dame Suzanne among her roses across the way. She must have clipped a hundred since noon. An hour ago Trezinie had seen the carriage from Les Cheniers pass by on its way to church with Mamzelle Euphraisie's pretty head looking like a picture enframed with the Easter lilies that filled the vehicle.

For the twentieth time Trezinie walked out upon the gallery. She saw M'sieur Michel and thought of the pine hill. When she thought of the hill she thought of the flowers that grew there—free as sunshine. The girl gave a joyous spring that changed to a farandole as her feet twinkled across the rough, loose boards of the gallery.

"He, Cami!" she cried, clapping her hands together.

Cami rose from the bench where he sat pegging away at the clumsy sole of a shoe, and came lazily to the fence that divided his abode from Trezinie's.

"Well, W'at?" he inquired with heavy amiability. She leaned far over the railing to better communicate with him.

"You'll go with me yonda on the hill to pick flowers fo' Easter, Cami? I'm goin' to take La Fringante along, too, to he'p with the baskets. W'at you say?"

"No!" was the stolid reply. "I'm boun' to finish them shoe', if it is fo' a nigga."

"Not now," she returned impatiently; "to-morrow mo'nin at sun-up. An' I tell you, Cami, my flowers'll beat all! Look yonda at 'Dame Suzanne pickin' her roses a'ready. An' Mamzelle Euphraisie she's car'ied her lilies an' gone, her. You tell me all that's goin' be fresh to-moro'!"

"Jus' like you say," agreed the boy, turning to resume his work. "But you want to mine out fo' the ole possum up in the wood. Let M'sieu Michel set eyes on you!" and he raised his arms as if aiming with a gun. "Pim, pam, poum! No mo' Trezinie, no mo' Cami, no mo' La Fringante—all stretch'!"

The possible risk which Cami so vividly foreshadowed but added a zest to Trezinie's projected excursion.

II.

It was hardly sun-up on the following morning when the three children—Trezinie, Cami and the little negress, La Fringante—were filling big, flat Indian baskets from the abundance of brilliant flowers that studded the hill.

In their eagerness they had ascended the slope and penetrated deep into the forest without thought of M'sieur Michel or of his abode. Suddenly, in the dense wood, they came upon his hut—low, forbidding, seeming to scowl rebuke upon them for their intrusion.

La Fringante dropped her basket, and, with a cry, fled. Cami looked as if he wanted to do the same. But Trezinie, after the first tremor, saw that the ogre himself was away. The wooden shutter of the one window was closed. The door, so low that even a small man must have stooped to enter it, was secured with a chain. Absolute silence reigned, except for the whirr of wings in the air, the fitful notes of a bird in the treetop.

"Can't you see it's nobody there!" cried Trezinie impatiently.

La Fringante, distracted between curiosity and terror, had crept cautiously back again. Then they all peeped through the wide chinks between the logs of which the cabin was built.

M'sieu Michel had evidently begun the construction of his house by felling a huge tree, whose remaining stump stood in the centre of the hut, and served him as a table. This primitive table was worn smooth by twenty-five years of use. Upon it were such humble utensils as the man required. Everything within the hovel, the sleeping bunk, the one seat, were as rude as a savage would have fashioned them.

The stolid Cami could have stayed for hours with his eyes fastened to the aperture, morbidly seeking some dead, mute sign of that awful pastime with which he believed M'sieur Michel was accustomed to beguile his solitude. But Trezinie was wholly possessed by the thought of her Easter offerings. She wanted flowers and flowers, fresh with the earth and crisp with dew.

When the three youngsters scampered down the hill again there was not a purple verbena left about M'sieur Michel's hut; not a May apple blossom, not a stalk of crimson phlox—hardly a violet.

He was something of a savage, feeling that the solitude belonged to him. Of late there had been forming within his soul a sentiment toward man, keener than indifference, bitter as hate. He was coming to dread even that brief intercourse with others into which his traffic forced him.

So when M'sieur Michel returned to his hut, and with his quick, accustomed eye saw that his woods had been despoiled, rage seized him. It was not that he loved the flowers that were gone more than he loved the stars, or the wind that trailed across the hill, but they belonged to and were a part of that life which he had made for himself, and which he wanted to live alone and unmolested.

Did not those flowers help him to keep his record of time that was passing? They had no right to vanish until the hot May days were upon him. How else should he know? Why had these people, with whom he had nothing in common, intruded upon his privacy and violated it? What would they not rob him of next?

He knew well enough it was Easter; he had heard and seen signs yesterday in the store that told him so. And he guessed that his woods had been rifled to add to the mummery of the day.

M'sieur Michel sat himself moodily down beside his table—centuries old—and brooded. He did not even notice his hounds that were pleading to be fed. As he revolved in his mind the event of the morning—innocent as it was in itself—it grew in importance and assumed a significance not at first apparent. He could not remain passive under pressure of its disturbance. He rose to his feet, every impulse aggressive, urging him to activity. He would go down among those people all gathered together, blacks and whites, and face them for once and all. He did not know what he would say to them, but it would be defiance—something to voice the hate that oppressed him.

The way down the hill, then across a piece of flat, swampy woodland and through the lane to the village was so familiar that it required no attention from him to follow it. His thoughts were left free to revel in the humor that had driven him from his kennel.

As he walked down the village street he saw plainly that the place was deserted save for the appearance of an occasional negress, who seemed occupied with preparing the midday meal. But about the church scores of horses were fastened; and M'sieur Michel could see that the edifice was thronged to the very threshold.

He did not once hesitate, but obeying the force that impelled him to face the people wherever they might be, he was soon standing with the crowd within the entrance of the church. His broad, robust shoulders had forced space for himself, and his leonine head stood higher than any there.

"Take off yo' hat!"

It was an indignant mulatto who addressed him. M'sieur Michel instinctively did as he was bidden. He saw confusedly that there was a mass of humanity close to him, whose contact and atmosphere affected him strangely. He saw his wild-flowers, too. He saw them plainly, in bunches and festoons, among the Easter Lilies and roses and geraniums. He was going to speak out, now; he had the right to and he would, just as soon as that clamor overhead would cease.

"Bonté divine! M'sieur Michel!" whispered 'Dame Suzanne tragically to her neighbor. Trezinie heard. Cami saw. They exchanged an electric glance, and tremblingly bowed their heads low.

M'sieur Michel looked wrathfully down at the puny mulatto who had ordered him to remove his hat. Why had he obeyed? That initial act of compliance had somehow weakened his will, his resolution. But he would regain his firmness just as soon as that clamor above gave him chance to speak.

It was the organ filling the small edifice with volumes of sound. It was the voices of men and women mingling in the "Gloria in excelsis Deo!"

The words bore no meaning for him apart from the old familiar strain which he had known as a child and chanted himself in that same organ-loft years ago. How it went on and on! Would it never cease! It was like a menace; like a voice reaching out from the dead past to taunt him.

"Gloria in excelsis Deo!" over and over! How the deep basso rolled it out! How the tenor and alto caught it up and passed it on to be lifted by the high, flute-like ring of the soprano, till all mingled again in the wild paean, "Gloria in excelsis!"

How insistent was the refrain! and where, what, was that mysterious, hidden quality in it; the power which was overcoming M'sieur Michel, stirring within him a turmoil that bewildered him?

There was no use in trying to speak, or in wanting to. His throat could not have uttered a sound. He wanted to escape, that was all. "Bonae voluntatis,"—he bent his head as if before a beating storm. "Gloria! Gloria! Gloria!" He must fly; he must save himself, regain his hill where sights and odors and sounds and saints or devils would cease to molest him. "In excelsis Deo!" He retreated, forcing his way backward to the door. He dragged his hat down over his eyes and staggered away down the road. But the refrain pursued him—"Pax! pax! pax!"—fretting him like a lash. He did not slacken his pace till the tones grew fainter than an echo, floating, dying away in an "in excelsis!" When he could hear it no longer he stopped and breathed a sigh of rest and relief.

III.

All day long M'sieur Michel stayed about his hut engaged in some familiar employment that he hoped might efface the unaccountable impressions of the morning. But his restlessness was unbounded. A longing had sprung up within him as sharp as pain and not to be appeased. At once, on this bright, warm Easter morning the voices that till now had filled his solitude became meaningless. He stayed mute and uncomprehending before them. Their significance had vanished before the driving want for human sympathy and companionship that had reawakened in his soul.

When night came on he walked through the woods down the slant of the hill again.

"It mus' be all fill' up with weeds," muttered M'sieur Michel to himself as he went. "Ah, Bon Dieu! with trees, Michel, with trees—in twenty-five years, man."

He had not taken the road to the village, but was pursuing a different one in which his feet had not walked for many days. It led him along the river bank for a distance. The narrow stream, stirred by the restless breeze, gleamed in the moonlight that was flooding the land.

As he went on and on, the scent of the new-plowed earth that had been from the first keenly perceptible, began to intoxicate him. He wanted to kneel and bury his face in it. He wanted to dig into it; turn it over. He wanted to scatter the seed again as he had done long ago, and watch the new, green life spring up as if at his bidding.

When he turned away from the river, and had walked a piece down the lane that divided Joe Duplan's plantation from that bit of land that had once been his, he wiped his eyes to drive away the mist that was making him see things as they surely could not be.

He had wanted to plant a hedge that time before he went away, but he had not done so. Yet there was the hedge before him, just as he had meant it to be, and filling the night with fragrance. A broad, low gate divided its length, and over this he leaned and looked before him in amazement. There were no weeds as he had fancied; no trees except the scattered live oaks that he remembered.

Could that row of hardy fig trees, old, squat and gnarled, be the twigs that he himself had set one day into the ground? One raw December day when there was a fine, cold mist falling. The chill of it breathed again upon him; the memory was so real. The land did not look as if it ever had been plowed for a field. It was a smooth, green meadow, with cattle huddled upon the cool sward, or moving with slow, stately tread as they nibbled the tender shoots.

There was the house unchanged, gleaming white in the moon, seeming to invite him beneath its calm shelter. He wondered who dwelt within it now. Whoever it was he would not have them find him, like a prowler, there at the gate. But he would come again and again like this at nighttime, to gaze and refresh his spirit.

A hand had been laid upon M'sieur Michel's shoulder and some one called his name. Startled, he turned to see who accosted him.

"Duplan!"

The two men who had not exchanged speech for so many years stood facing each other for a long moment in silence.

"I knew you would come back some day, Michel. It was a long time to wait, but you have come home at last."

M'sieur Michel cowered instinctively and lifted his hands with expressive deprecatory gesture. "No, no; it's no place for me, Joe; no place!"

"Isn't a man's home a place for him, Michel?" It seemed less a question than an assertion, charged with gentle authority.

"Twenty-five years, Duplan; twenty-five years! It's no use; it's too late."

"You see, I have used it," went on the planter, quietly, ignoring M'sieur Michel's protestations. "Those are my cattle grazing off there. The house has served me many a time to lodge guests or workmen, for whom I had no room at Les Cheniers. I have not exhausted the soil with any crops. I had not the right to do that. Yet am I in your debt, Michel, and ready to settle en bon ami."

The planter had opened the gate and entered the inclosure, leading M'sieur Michel with him. Together they walked toward the house.

Language did not come readily to either—one so unaccustomed to hold intercourse with men; both so stirred with memories that would have rendered any speech painful. When they had stayed long in a silence which was eloquent of tenderness, Joe Duplan spoke:

"You know how I tried to see you, Michel, to speak with you, and you never would."

M'sieur Michel answered with but a gesture that seemed a supplication.

"Let the past all go, Michel. Begin your new life as if the twenty-five years that are gone had been a long night, from which you have only awakened. Come to me in the morning," he added with quick resolution, "for a horse and a plow." He had taken the key of the house from his pocket and placed it in M'sieur Michel's hand.

"A horse?" M'sieur Michel repeated uncertainly; "a plow! Oh, it's too late, Duplan; too late."

"It isn't too late. The land has rested all these years, man; it's fresh, I tell you; and rich as gold. Your crop will be the finest in the land." He held out his hand and M'sieur Michel pressed it without a word in reply, save a muttered "Mon ami."

Then he stood there watching the planter disappear behind the high, clipped hedge.

He held out his arms. He could not have told if it was toward the retreating figure, or in welcome to an infinite peace that seemed to descend upon him and envelop him.

All the land was radiant except the hill far off that was in black shadow against the sky.

POEM FOR GRANVILLE IVANHOE JORDAN
November 4, 1890–December 21, 1974
Dedicated to Stephen Henderson

June Jordan

I

At the top of your tie
the dressy maroon number
with one/small
gravy stain
remaining

the knot is now too narrow for your neck

a ridiculous a dustfree/shiny box confines
your arms and legs
accustomed to a boxer's hunch a wrestler's hauling
energies at partial rest

3 or 4 A.M. a thousand nights
who stubbornly retrieved your own
into
illumination
            bright beyond blindfiling of
            a million letters at the Post Office which
            never forwarded even one
            of a hundred
            fantasies
            your kitchenkept plans
keeping you awake

West Indian in kitchen exile
alone between the days
and studying the National Geographic Magazines
white explorations and
excitement
in the places you were forced to leave

                              no shoes
                              no teeth

but oxlike shoulders
and hazel eyes that watered
slightly
from the reading you did teach yourself to do

West Indian in kitchen exile
omnivorous consumer of thick
kitchen table catalogs
of seeds for sale
for red
bright flowers

seeds

slick and colorful
on the quick
lush pages
advertising pear and
apple trees
or peaches
in first bloom

                who saved for money orders
                for the flowers
                for the trees
                who used a spade
                and shovel
                heavily and well
                to plant the Brooklyn backyard
                innocent of all
                the succulent
                the gorgeous schemes
                you held between your fingers
                like a simple
                piece of paper

Jesus, Daddy
what did you expect

an orange grove
a eucalyptus
roses

from the cities that despised the sweet calypso
of your trust?

II

Who stole the mustache from your face?
It's gone.
Who took it away?
Why did you stop there

                    on your knees

at eighty four

                    a man

down on your knees

                    in inconceivable but willing
                    prayer/your life
                    God's baby in gray hair

What pushed you from your own two feet?

                    my father

III

To this you have come

                    a calm a concrete pit

contains your corpse
above the spumespent ending of the surf
against the mountain trees and fertile pitch
of steeply clinging dirt

                    "Sleep on Beloved
                    Take Thy Rest"

the minister
eyes bare beneath the island light
intones a feeling mumbo jumbo

> *"ashes to ashes*
> *dust to dust"*

the village men
wrists strained to lumped up veins and cartilage
(from carrying the casket)
do not pray
they do not sing

> *"A-bide with me,*
> *fast falls the eventide"*

It's afternoon
It's hot
It's lit by sun that cannot be undone

by death

MY FATHER IN THE NAVY: A CHILDHOOD MEMORY

Judith Ortiz Cofer

Stiff and immaculate
in the white cloth of his uniform
and a round cap on his head like a halo,
he was an apparition on leave from a shadow-world
and only flesh and blood when he rose from below
the waterline where he kept watch over the engines
and dials making sure the ship parted the waters
on a straight course.
Mother, brother and I kept vigil
on the nights and dawns of his arrivals,
watching the corner beyond the neon sign of a quasar
for the flash of white our father like an angel
heralding a new day.
His homecomings were the verses
we composed over the years making up
the siren's song that kept him coming back from the bellies of iron whales
and into our nights
like the evening prayer.

THE GILDED SIX BITS

Zora Neale Hurston

It was a Negro yard around a Negro house in a Negro settlement that looked to the payroll of the G and G Fertilizer works for its support.

But there was something happy about the place. The front yard was parted in the middle by a sidewalk from gate to doorstep, a sidewalk edged on either side by quart bottles driven neck down to the ground on a slant. A mess of homey flowers planted without a plan but blooming cheerily from their helter-skelter places. The fence and house were whitewashed. The porch and steps scrubbed white.

The front door stood open to the sunshine so that the floor of the front room could finish drying after its weekly scouring. It was Saturday. Everything clean from the front gate to the privy house. Yard raked so that the strokes of the rake would make a pattern. Fresh newspaper cut in fancy-edge on the kitchen shelves.

Missie May was bathing herself in the galvanized washtub in the bedroom. Her dark-brown skin glistened under the soapsuds that skittered down from her wash rag. Her stiff young breasts thrust forward aggressively like broad-based cones with the tips lacquered in black.

She heard men's voices in the distance and glanced at the dollar clock on the dresser.

"Humph! Ah'm way behind time t'day! Joe gointer be heah 'fore Ah git mah clothes on if Ah don't make haste."

She grabbed the clean meal sack at hand and dried herself hurriedly and began to dress. But before she could tie her slippers, there came the ring of singing metal on wood. Nine times.

Missie May grinned with delight. She had not seen the big tall man come stealing in the gate and creep up the walk grinning happily at the joyful mischief he was about to commit. But she knew that it was her husband throwing silver dollars in the door for her to pick up and pile beside her plate at dinner. It was this way every Saturday afternoon. The nine dollars hurled into the open door, he scurried to a hiding place behind the cape jasmine bush and waited.

Missie May promptly appeared at the door in mock alarm.

"Who dat chunkin' money in mah do'way?" she demanded. No answer from the yard. She leaped off the porch and hung over the gate to look up and down the road. While she did this, the man behind the jasmine darted to the chinaberry tree. She spied him and gave chase.

"Nobody ain't gointer be chunkin' money at me and Ah not do'me nothin'," she shouted in mock anger. He ran around the house with Missie May at his heels. She overtook him at the kitchen door. He ran inside but could not close it after him before she crowded in and locked with him in a rough and tumble. For several minutes the two were a furious mass of male and female energy.

Shouting, laughing, twisting, turning, and Joe trying, but not too hard, to get away.

"Missie May, tak yo' hand out mah pocket!" Joe shouted out between laughs.

"Ah ain't, Joe, not lessen you gwine gimme whateve' it is good you got in yo' pocket. Turn it go Joe, do Ah'll tear you' clothes."

"Go on tear 'em. You de one dat pushes de needles round heah. Move yo' hand Missie May."

"Lemme git dat paper sack out yo' pocket. Ah bet its candy kisses."

"Tain't. Move yo hand. Woman ain't got no business in a man's clothes nohow. Go 'way."

Missie May gouged way down and gave an upward jerk and triumphed.

"Unhhunh! Ah got it. It 'tis so candy kisses. Ah knowed you had somethin' for me in yo' clothes. Now Ah got to see whut's in every pocket you got."

Joe smiled indulgently and let his wife go through all of his pockets and take out the things that he had hidden there for her to find. She bore off the chewing gum, the cake of sweet soap, the pocket handkerchief as if she had wrested them from him, as if they had not been bought for the sake of this friendly battle.

"Whew! dat play-fight done got me all warmed up," Joe exclaimed. "Got me some water in de kittle?"

"Yo' water is on de fire and yo' clean things is cross de bed. Hurry up and wash yo'self and git changed so we kin eat. Ah'm hongry." As Missie said this, she bore the steaming kettle into the bedroom.

"You ain't hongry, sugar," Joe contradicted her. "Youse jes's little empty. Ah'm de one whut's hongry. Ah could eat up camp meetin', back off 'ssociation, and drink Jurdan dry. Have it on de table when Ah git out de tub."

"Don't you mess wid mah business, man. You git in yo' clothes. Ah'm a real wife, not no dress and breath. Ah might not look lak one, but if you burn me, you won't git a thing but wife ashes."

Joe splashed in the bedroom and Missie May fanned around in the kitchen. A fresh red and white checked cloth on the table. Big pitcher of buttermilk beaded with pale drops of butter from the churn. Hot fried mullet, crackling bread, ham hocks atop a mound of string beans and new potatoes, and perched on the window-sill a pone of spicy potato pudding.

Very little talk during the meal but that little consisted of banter that pretended to deny affection but in reality flaunted it. Like when Missie May reached for a second helping of the tater pone. Joe snatched it out of her reach. After Missie May had made two or three unsuccessful grabs at the pan, she begged, "Aw, Joe gimme some mo' dat tater pone."

"Nope, sweetenin' is for us men'folks. Y'all pritty li'l frail eels don't need nothin' lak dis. You too sweet already."

"Please, Joe."

"Naw, naw. Ah don't want you to git no sweeter that whut you is already. We goin' down de road al li'l piece t'night so you go put on yo' Sunday-go-to-meetin' things."

Missie May looked at her husband to see if he was playing some prank. "Sho' nuff, Joe?"

"Yeah. We goin' to de ice cream parlor."

"Where de ice cream parlor at, Joe?"

"A new man done come heah from Chicago and he done got a place and took and opened it up for a ice cream parlor, and bein' as it's real swell, Ah wants you to be one de first ladies to walk in dere and have some set down."

"Do Jesus, Ah ain't knowed nothin' 'bout it. Who de man done it?"

"Mister Otis D. Slemmons, of spots and places—Memphis, Chicago, Jacksonville, Philadelphia and so on."

"Dat heavy-set man wid his mouth full of gold teethes?"

"Yeah. Where did you see 'im at?"

"Ah went down to de sto' tuh git a box of lye and Ah seen 'im standin' on de corner talkin' to some of de mens, and Ah come on back and went to scrubbin' de floor, and he passed and tipped his hat whilst Ah was scourin' de steps. Ah thought never Ah seen him befo'."

Joe smiled pleasantly. "Yeah, he's up to date. He got de finest clothes Ah ever seen on a colored man's back."

"Aw, he don't look no better in his clothes than you do in yourn. He got a puzzlegut on 'im and he so chuckle-headed, he got a pone behind his neck."

Joe looked down at his own abdomen and said wistfully, "Wisht Ah had a build on me lak he got. He ain't puzzlegutted, honey. He jes' got a corperation. Dat make 'm look lak a rich white man. All rich mens is got some belly on 'em."

"Ah seen de pitchers of Henry Ford and he's a spare-built man and Rockefeller look lak he ain't got but one gut. But Ford and Rockefeller and dis Slemmons and all de rest kin be as many-gutted as dey please, ah'm satisfied wid you jes' lak you is baby. God took pattern after a pine tree and built you noble. Youse a pretty still man, and if Ah knowed any way to make you mo' pretty still Ah'd take and do it."

Joe reached over gently and toyed with Missie May's ear. "You jes' say dat cause you love me, but Ah know Ah can't hold no light to Otis D. Slemmons. Ah ain't never been nowhere and Ah ain't got nothin' but you."

"How you know dat, Joe."

"He tole us so hisself."

"Dat don't make it so. His mouf is cut cross-ways, ain't it? Well, he kin lie jes lak anybody els."

"Good Lawd, Missie! You womens sho' is hard to sense into things. He's got a five-dollar gold piece for a stick-pin and he got a ten-dollar gold piece on his watch chain and his mouf is jes' crammed full of gold teethes. Sho' wisht it wuz mine. And whut make it so cool, he got money 'cumulated. And womens give it all to 'im."

"Ah don't see whut de womens see on 'im. Ah wouldn't give 'im a wind if de sherff wuz after 'im."

"Well, he tole us how de white womens in Chicago give 'im all dat gold money. So he don't 'low nobody to touch it at all. Not even put dey finger on it. Dey tole 'im not to. You kin make 'miration at it, but don't tetch it."

"Whyn't he stay up dere where dey so crazy 'bout 'im?"

"Ah reckon dey done made 'im vast-rich and he wants to travel some. He say dey wouldn't leave 'im hit a lick of work. He got mo' lady people crazy 'bout him than he kin shake a stick at."

"Joe, Ah hates to see you so dumb. Dat stray nigger jes' tell y'all anything and y'all b'lieve it."

"Go 'head on now, honey and put on yo' clothes. He talkin' 'bout his pritty womens—Ah want 'im to see mine."

Missie May went off to dress and Joe spent the time trying to make his stomach punch out like Slemmons' middle. He tried the rolling swagger of the stranger, but found that his tall bone-and-muscle stride fitted ill with it. He just had time to drop back into his seat before Missie May came dressed to go.

On the way home that night Joe was exultant. "Didn't Ah say ole Otis was swell? Can't he talk Chicago talk? Wazn't dat funny whut he said when great big fat ole Ida Armstrong come in? He asted me, "'Who is dat broad wid de forty shake?' Dat's a new word. Us always thought forty was a set of figgers but he showed us where it means a whole heap of things. Sometimes he don't say forty, he jes' say thirty-eight and two and dat mean de same thing. Know whut he tole me when Ah was payin' for our ice cream? He say, 'Ah have to hand it to you, Joe. Dat wife of yours is jes thirty-eight and two. Yessuh, she's forty!' Ain't he killin?"

"He'll do in case of a rush. But he sho' is got uh heap uh gold on 'im. Dat's de first time Ah ever seed gold money. It lookted good on him sho' nuff, but it'd look a whole heap better on you."

"Who, me? Missie May was youse crazy! Where would a po' man lak me git gold money from?"

Missie May was silent for a minute, then she said, "Us might find some goin' long de road some time. Us could."

"Who would be losin' gold money 'round heah? We ain't even seen none dese white folks wearin' no gold money on dey watch chain. You must be figgeren' Mister Packard or Mister Cadillac goin' pass through heah . . ."

"You don't know whut been lost 'round heah. Maybe somebody way back in memorial times lost they gold money and went on off and it ain't never been found. And then if we wuz to find it, you could wear some 'thout havin' no gang of womens lak dat Slemmons say he got."

Joe laughed and hugged her. "Don't be so wishful 'bout me. Ah'm satisfied de way Ah is. So long as Ah be yo' husband, ah don't keer 'bout nothin' else. Ah'd ruther all de other womens in de world to be dead than for you to have de toothache. Less we go to bed and git our night rest."

It was Saturday night once more before Joe could parade his wife in Slemmons' ice cream parlor again. He worked the night shift and Saturday was his only night off. Every other evening around six o'clock he left home, and dying dawn saw him hustling home around the lake where the challenging sun flung a flaming sword from east to west across the trembling water.

That was the best part of life—going home to Missie May. Their whitewashed house, the mock battle on Saturday, the dinner and ice cream parlor afterwards, church on Sunday nights when Missie outdressed any woman in town—all, everything was right.

One night around eleven the acid ran out at the G and G. The foreman knocked off the crew and let the steam die down. As Joe rounded the lake on his way home, a lean moon rode the lake in a silver boat. If anybody had asked Joe about the moon on the lake, he would have said he hadn't paid it any attention. But he saw it with his feelings. It made him yearn painfully for Missie. Creation obsessed him. He thought about children. They had been married for more than a year now. They had money put away. They ought to be making little feet for shoes. A little boy child would be about right.

He saw a dim light in the bedroom and decided to come in through the kitchen door. He could wash the fertilizer dust off himself before presenting himself to Missie May. It would be nice for her not to know that he was there until he slipped into his place in bed and hugged her back. She always liked that.

He eased the kitchen door open slowly and silently, but when he went to set his dinner bucket on the table he bumped it into a pile of dishes, and something crashed to the floor. He heard his wife gasp in fright and hurried to reassure her.

"Iss me, honey. Don't get skeered."

There was a quick, large movement in the bedroom. A rustle, a thud, and a stealthy silence. The light went out.

What? Robbers? Murderers? Some varmint attacking his helpless wife, perhaps. He struck a match, threw himself on guard and stepped over the door-sill into the bedroom.

The great belt on the wheel of Time slipped and eternity stood still. By the match light he could see the man's legs fighting with his breeches in his frantic desire to get them on. He had both chance and time to kill the intruder in his helpless condition—half-in and half-out of his pants—but he was too weak to take action. The shapeless enemies of humanity that live in the hours of Time waylaid Joe. He was assaulted in his weakness. Like Samson awakening after his haircut. So he just opened his mouth and laughed.

The match went out and he struck another and lit the lamp. A howling wind raced across his heart, but underneath its fury he heard his wife sobbing and Slemmons pleading for his life. Offering to buy it with all that he had. "Please, suh, don't kill me. Sixty-two dollars at de sto' gold money."

Joe just stood. Slemmons looked at the window, but it was screened. Joe stood out like a rough-backed mountain between him and the door. Barring him from escape, from sunrise, from life.

He considered a surprise attack upon the big clown that stood there laughing like a chessy cat. But before his fist could travel an inch, Joe's own rushed out to crush him like a battering ram. Then Joe stood over him.

"Git into yo' damn rags, Slemmons, and dat quick."

Slemmons scrambled to his feet and into his vest and coat. As he grabbed his hat, Joe's fury overrode his intentions and he grabbed at Slemmons with his left hand and struck at him with his right. The right landed. The left grazed the front of his vest. Slemmons was knocked a somersault into the kitchen and fled through the open door. Joe found himself alone with Missie May, with the golden watch charm clutched in his left fist. A short bit of broken chain dangled between his fingers.

Missie May was sobbing. Wails of weeping without words. Joe stood, and after awhile she found out that he had something in his hand. And then he stood and felt without thinking and without seeing with his natural eyes. Missie May kept on crying and Joe kept on feeling so much and not knowing what to do with all his feelings, he put Slemmons' watch charm in his pants pocket and took a good laugh and went to bed.

"Missie May, whut you crying for?"

"Cause Ah love you so hard and Ah know you don't love me no mo.'"

Joe sank his face into the pillow for a spell then he said huskily, "You don't know de feelings of dat yet, Missie May."

"Oh Joe, honey, he said he wuz gointer gimme dat gold money and he jes' kept on after me—"

Joe was very still and silent for a long time. Then he said, "Well, don't cry no mo', Missie May. Ah got yo' gold piece for you."

The hours went past on their rusty ankles. Joe still and quiet on one bed-rail and Missie May wrung dry of sobs on the other. Finally the sun's tide crept upon the shore of night and drowned all its hours. Missie May with her face stiff and streaked towards the window saw the dawn come into her yard. It was day. Nothing more. Joe wouldn't be coming home as usual. No need to fling open the front door and sweep off the porch, making it nice for Joe. Never no more breakfast to cook; no more washing and starching of Joe's jumper-jackets and pants. No more nothing. So why get up?

With this strange man in her bed, she felt embarrassed to get up and dress. She decided to wait till he had dressed and gone. Then she would get up, dress quickly and be gone forever beyond reach of Joe's looks and laughs. But he never moved. Red light turned to yellow, then white.

From beyond the no-man's land between them came a voice. A strange voice that yesterday had been Joe's.

"Missie May, ain't you gonna fix me no breakfus'?"

She sprang out of bed. "Yeah, Joe. Ah didn't reckon you wuz hongry."

No need to die today. Joe needed her for a few more minutes anyhow.

Soon there was a roaring fire in the cook stove. Water bucket full of two chickens killed. Joe loved fried chicken and rice. She didn't deserve a thing and good Joe was letting her cook him some breakfast. She rushed hot biscuits to the table as Joe took his seat.

He ate with his eyes on his plate. No laughter, no banter.

"Missie May, you ain't eatin' yo' breakfus'."

"Ah don't choose none, Ah thank yuh."

His coffee cup was empty. She sprang to refill it. When she turned from the stove and bent to set the cup beside Joe's plate, she saw the yellow coin on the table between them.

She slumped into her seat and wept into her arms.

Presently Joe said calmly, "Missie May, you cry too much. Don't look back lak Lot's wife and turn to salt."

The sun, the hero of every day, the impersonal old man that beams as brightly on death as on birth, came up every morning and raced across the blue dome and dipped into the sea of fire every evening. Water ran down hill and birds nested.

Missie knew why she didn't leave Joe. She couldn't. She loved him too much. But she couldn't understand why Joe didn't leave her. He was polite, even kind at times, but aloof.

There were no more Saturday romps. No ringing silver dollars to stack beside her plate. No pockets to rifle. In fact the yellow coin in his trousers was like a monster hiding in the cave of his pockets to destroy her.

She often wondered if he still had it, but nothing could have induced her to ask nor yet to explore his pockets to see for herself. Its shadow was in the house whether or no.

One night Joe came home around midnight and complained of pains in the back. He asked Missie to rub him down with liniment. It had been three months since Missie had touched his body and it all seemed strange. But she rubbed him. Grateful for the chance. Before morning, youth triumphed and Missie exulted. But the next day, as she joyfully made up their bed, beneath her pillow she found the piece of money with the bit of chain attached.

Alone to herself, she looked at the thing with loathing, but look she must. She took it into her hands with trembling and saw first thing that it was no gold piece. It was a gilded half-dollar. Then she knew why Slemmons had forbidden anyone to touch his gold. He trusted village eyes at a distance not to recognize his stick-pin as a gilded quarter, and his watch charm as a four-bit piece.

She was glad at first that Joe had left it there. Perhaps he was through with her punishment. They were man and wife again. Then another thought came clawing at her. He had come home to buy from her as if she were any woman in the long house. Fifty cents for her love. As if to say that he could pay as well as Slemmons. She slid the coin into his Sunday pants pocket and dressed herself and left his house.

Halfway between her house and the quarters she met her husband's mother, and after a short talk she turned and went back home. If she had not the substance of marriage, she had the outside show. Joe must leave her. She let him see she didn't want his old gold four-bits too.

She saw no more of the coin for some time though she knew that Joe could not help finding it in his pocket. But his health kept poor, and he came home at least every ten days to be rubbed.

The sun swept around the horizon, trailing its robes of weeks and days. One morning as Joe came in from work, he found Missie May chopping wood. Without a word he took the ax and chopped a huge pile before he stopped.

"You ain't got no business choppin' wood, and you know it."

"How come? Ah been choppin' it for de last longest."

"Ah ain't blind. You makin' feet for shoes."

"Won't you be glad to have a li'l baby chile, Joe?"

"You know dat 'thout astin' me."

"Iss gointer be a boy chile and de very spit of you."

"You reckon, Missie May?"

"Who else could it look lak?"

Joe said nothing, but he thrust his hand deep into his pocket and fingered something there.

It was almost six months later Missie May took to bed and Joe went and got his mother to come wait on the house.

Missie May delivered a fine boy. Her travail was over when Joe came in from work one morning. His mother and the old women were drinking great bowls of coffee around the fire in the kitchen.

The minute Joe came into the room his mother called him aside.

"How did Missie May make out?" he asked quickly.

"Who, dat gal? She strong as a ox. She gointer have plenty mo'. We done fixed her wid de sugar and lard to sweeten her for de nex' one."

Joe stood silent awhile.

"You ain't ast 'bout de baby, Joe. You oughter be mighty proud cause he sho' is de spittin' image of yuh, son. Dat's yourn all right, if you never git another one, dat un is yourn. And you know Ah'm mighty proud too, son, cause Ah never thought well of you marrin' Missie May cause her ma used tuh fan her foot 'round right smart and Ah been mighty skeered dat Missie May wuz gointer git misput on her road."

Joe said nothing. He fooled around the house till late in the day then just before he went to work, he went and stood at the foot of the bed and asked his wife how she felt. He did this every day during the week.

On Saturday he went to Orlando to make his market. It had been a long time since he had done that.

Meat and lard, meal and flour, soap and starch. Cans of corn and tomatoes. All the staples. He fooled around town for awhile and bought bananas and apples.

Way after while he went around to the candy store.

"Hellow, Joe," the clerk greeted him. "Aint' seen you in a long time."

"Nope, Ah ain't been heah. Been 'round spots and places."

"Want some of them molasses kisses you always buy?"

"Yessuh." He threw the gilded half-dollar on the counter. "Will dat spend?"

"Whut is it, Joe? Well, I'll be doggone! A gold-plated four-bit piece. Where'd you git it, Joe?"

"Offen a stray nigger dat come through Eatonville. He had it on his watch chain for a charm—goin' 'round making out iss gold money. Ha ha! He had a quarter on his tie pin and it wuz all golded up too. Tryin' to fool people. Makin' out he so rich and everything. Ha! Ha! Tryin' to tole off folkses wives from home."

"How did you git it, Joe? Did he fool you, too?"

"Who me? Naw suh! He ain't fooled me none. Know whut Ah done? He come 'round me wid his smart talk. Ah hauled off and knocked 'im down and took his old four-bits 'way from 'im. Gointer buy my wife some good ole 'lasses kisses wid it. Gimme fifty cents worth of dem candy kisses."

"Fifty cents buys a mightly lot of candy kisses, Joe. Why don't you split it up and take some chocolate bars, too. They eat good, too."

"Yessuh, dey do, but Ah wants all dat in kisses. Ah got a li'l boy chile home now. Tain't a week old yet, but he kin suck a sugar tit and maybe eat one them kisses hisself."

Joe got his candy and left the store. The clerk turned to the next customer. "Wisht I could be like these darkies. Laughin' all the time. Nothin' worries 'em."

Back in Eatonville, Joe reached his own front door. There was the ring of singing metal on wood. Missie May couldn't run to the door, but she crept there as quickly as she could.

"Joe Banks, Ah hear you chunkin' money in mah do'way. You wait till Ah get mah strength back and Ah'm gointer fix you for dat."

A TENDER MAN

Toni Cade Bambara

The girl was sitting in the booth, one leg wrapped around the other cartoon-like. Knee socks drooping, panties peeping from her handbag, ears straining from her head for the soft crepe footfalls, straining less Aisha silent and sudden catch her unawares with the dirty news.

She hadn't caught Cliff's attention. His eyes were simply at rest in that direction. And nothing better to do, he had designed a drama of her. His eyes resting on that booth, on that swivel chair, waiting for Aisha to return and fill it. When the chatty woman in the raincoat had been sitting where the nervous girl sat now, Aisha had flashed him a five-minute sign. That was fifteen minutes ago.

He hadn't known he'd mind the waiting. But he'd been feeling preoccupied of late, off-center, anxious even. Thought he could shrug it off, whatever it was. But sitting on the narrow folding chair waiting, nothing to arrest his attention and focus him, he felt crowded by something too heavy to shrug off. He decided he was simply nervous about the impending student takeover.

He flipped through a tattered *Ebony*, pausing at pictures of children, mothers and children, couples and children, grandparents and children. But no father and child. It was a conspiracy, he chuckled to himself, to keep fathers—he searched for a word—outside. He flipped through the eligible bachelors of the years, halting for a long time at the photo of Carl Davis, his ole army mate who'd nearly deserted in the spring of '61. He was now with RCA making $20,000 a year. Cliff wondered doing what.

The girl was picking her face, now close to panic. In a moment she would bolt for the door. He could imagine heads lifting, swiveling, perfect strangers providing each other with hairy explanations. He could hear the women tsk-tsking, certain that their daughters would never. Aisha came through the swinging doors and he relaxed, not realizing till that moment how far he had slipped into the girl's drama. Aisha shot three fingers in his direction and he nodded. The girl was curled up tight now, Cliff felt her tension, staring at the glass slide Aisha slid onto the table. She leaned over the manila folder Aisha opened, hand screening the side of her face as though to block the people out. She was crying. The sobbing audible, though muffled now that the screening hand was doubled up in her mouth. Cliff was uncomfortable amongst so many women and this young one crying. Cliff got up to look for the water fountain.

Up and down the corridors folks walked distractedly, clutching slips of colored papers. A few looked terror-struck, like models for the covers of the books he often found his students buried in. Glancing at the slips of green or white, checking them against the signs on the doors, each had a particular style with the entrance, he noted. Knocking timidly, shivering, Judgment Day. Turning knobs stealthily and looking about, second-story types. Brisk entrances with caps yanked low, yawl deal with me, shit. Cliff moved in and out among the paper-slip clutchers, doorway handlers, teen-agers pulling younger brothers and sisters along, older folk pausing to read the posters. The walls were lined with posters urging VD tests, Pap smears, examinations painless and confidential. In less strident Technicolor, others argued the joys of planned parenthood.

Cliff approached the information desk, for the sister on the switchboard seemed to be wearing two wigs at once and he had to see that. The guard leaned way back before considering his question about the water fountain, stepped away from a woman leaning over the desk inquiring after a clinic, gave wide berth to all the folk who entered and headed in that direction, then pointed out the water fountain, backed up against the desk in a dramatic recoil. Cliff smiled at first and considered fucking with the dude, touching him, maybe drooling a bit on his uniform. But he moved off, feeling unclean.

At the water fountain a young father hoisted his daughter too far into the spout. Cliff held the button down and the brother smiled relief, a two-handed grip centering now the little girl, who gurgled and horsed around in the water, then held a jaw full even after she was put down on the floor again.

"This place is a bitch, ain't it?" The brother nodding vigorous agreement to his own remark.

"My wife's visiting her folks and I'm about to lose my mind with these kids." He smiled proudly, though, jutting his chin in the direction of the rest of his family. Two husky boys around eight and ten were doing base slides in the upper corridor.

"Man, if I had the clap, I sure as hell wouldn't come here for no treatments." His frown made Cliff look around. In that moment the lights seem to dim, the paint job age, the posters slump. A young girl played hopscotch in the litter, her mother pushing her along impatiently.

Yeh, a bitch, Cliff had meant to say, but all that came out was a wheezy mumble.

"My ole lady says to me 'go to the clinic and pick up my pills.' Even calls me long distance to remind me she's running out. 'Don't forget to get the pills, B.J.' So I come to get the damn pills, right?" He ran his hand through his bush, gripping a fistful and tossing his head back and forth. "Man oh man," he groaned, shaking his head by the hair. The gesture had started out as a simple self-caress, had moved swiftly into an I-don't-believe-this-shit nod, and before Cliff knew it, the brother'd become some precinct victim, his head bam-bam against the walls. "Man oh man, this crazy-ass place! Can't even get a word in for the 'What's your clinic number?' 'Where's your card?' 'Have you seen the cashier?' 'Have you got insurance?' 'Are you on the welfare?' 'Do you have a yellow slip?' 'Where's your card?' 'Who's ya mama?' Phwweeoo! I'm goin straight to the drugstore and get me a crate of rubbers right on. I ain't puttin my woman through this shit."

"Daddy." The little girl was yanking on his pants leg for attention. When she got it, she made a big X in the air.

"Oh, right. I forgot. Sorry, baby." He turned to Cliff and shrugged in mock sheepishness. "Gotta watch ya mouth round these kids these days, they get on ya. Stay on my cause bout the smoking, can't even bring a poke chop in the house, gotta sneak a can of beer and step out on the fire escape to smoke the dope. Man, these kids sompthin!" He was starting that vigorous nodding again, watching his sons approach. Cliff couldn't keep his eyes off the brother's bobbing head. It reminded him of Granddaddy Mobley so long ago, play horsy, whinnying down the hallway of Miss Hazel's boardinghouse, that head going a mile a minute and his sister Alma riding high, whipping her horse around the head and shoulders and laughing so hard Miss Hazel threatened to put them out.

"Yeh," he was sighing, nudging Cliff less he miss the chance to dig on the two young dudes coming, punching invisible catcher's mitts, diddyboppin like their daddy must've done it years before. "Later for them pills, anyway. It's back to good old reliable Trojans."

"Pills dangerous," Cliff said.

"Man, just living is a danger. And every day. Every day, man."

"We going to the poolroom now?" the older boy was asking, nodding first to Cliff.

"I want some Chinese food." The younger seemed to be addressing this to Cliff, shifting his gaze to his father long after he'd finished speaking.

"Hold it, youngbloods. Hold on a damn minute. I gotta catch me some sleep and get to work in a coupla hours. Yawl bout to wear my ass out."

"Daddy."

"Oh damn, I'm sorry. Sorry." The brother made two huge X's in the air and dropped his head shamefaced till his daughter laughed.

"Man, you got kids?"

"Yeah" was all Cliff said, not sure what else he could offer. It had been pleasant up to then, the brother was easy to be easy with. But now he seemed to be waiting for Cliff to share what Cliff wasn't sure he had to share. He bent to take a drink. "Daughter," he offered, trying to calculate her age. He'd always used the Bay of Pigs invasion as a guide.

"They sompthin, ain't they?" the brother broke in, his children dragging him off to the door. "Take it slow, my man."

Cliff nodded and bent for another drink. Bay of Pigs was the spring of '61. His daughter had been born that summer. He bit his lip. Hell, how many fathers could just tick off the ages of their children, right off the bat? Not many. But then if the brother had put the question to him, as Aisha had the day before—What sort of person is your daughter?—Cliff would not have known how to answer. He let the water bubble up against closed lips for a while, not sure what the fact said about the man he was, or at least had thought he was, hoped he was, had planned to be for so long, was convinced when still a boy he could be once he got out of that house of worrisome women.

Aisha had come quietly up behind him and linked arms. "Hey, mister," she cooed, "how bout taking a po' colored gal to dinner." She pulled him away from the water fountain. "I'm starving."

Starving. Cliff looked at her quickly, but she did not react. Starving. He stared at her, but she was checking the buttons on her blouse, then stepping back for him to catch the door. She moved out swiftly and down the stairs ahead of him, not so much eager to get away, for she'd said how much she liked her job at the clinic. But eager to be done with it for the day and be with him. She waited at the foot of the stairs and linked arms again.

Cliff smiled. He dug her. Had known her less than a week, but felt he knew her. A chick who dealt straight up. No funny changes to go through. He liked the way she made it clear that she dug him.

"Whatcha grinnin about?" she asked, adjusting her pace to his. She was a brisk walker—he had remarked on it the day before—Northern urban brisk. I bet you like to lead too when you dance, he had teased her.

"Thinking about the first time I called you," he said.

"Oh? Oh." She nodded and was done, as though in that split second she had retrieved the tape from storage, played it, analyzed his version of what went down, and knew exactly what he had grinned about and that was that. He had kidded her about that habit too. "You mean the way I push for clarity, honesty?"

That was what he had meant, but he didn't like the cocky way she said it with the phony questions mark on the end. She was a chick who'd been told she was too hard, too sure, too swift, and had made adjustments here and there, softening the edges. He wasn't sure that was honest of her, though he'd never liked women with hard edges.

"No," he half-lied. "Your sensitivity. I like the way you said after turning me down for a drink, 'Hey, Brother—'"

"I called you Cliff. I'm not interested in being your sister."

He hugged her arm. "Okay, 'Hey, Cliff,' you said, 'I ain't rejecting you, but I don't drink, plus I got to get up at the crack of dawn tomorrow to prepare for a workshop. How about dinner instead?'"

"And that tickles you?"

"It refreshes me," he said, laughing, feeling good. It wasn't so easy being a dude, always putting yourself out there to be rejected. He'd never much cared for aggressive women; on the other hand, he appreciated those who met him halfway. He slowed her down some more. "Hey, city girl," he drawled. "This here a country boy you walkin' wid, ain't used to shoes yet. The restaurant'll be there. Don't close till late."

"I'm starving, fool. Come on and feed me. You can take off them shoes. I'll carry em."

He hugged her arm and picked up his pace. It was silly, he told himself, these endless control games he liked to play with assertive types. He was feeling too good. But then he wasn't. Starving. She had raised that question: Can you swear no child of yours is starving to death? Not confronting him or even asking him, softening the edges, but addressing the workshop, reading off a list of questions that might get the discussion started. The brother next to him had slapped his knees with his cap and muttered, "Here we go again with some women lib shit." But a sister across the aisle had been more vocal, jumping up to say, "Run it down to the brothers. Let's just put them other questions on hold and stay with this one a while," she demanded. "Yeah, can you swear?" Her hot eyes sweeping the room. "Can you deal with that, you men in here? Can you deal with that one?"

The discussion got sidetracked, it'd seemed to Cliff at the time. Everybody talking at once, all up in each other's face. Paternity, birth control, genocide, responsibility, fathering, mothering, children, child support, warrants, the courts, prison. One brother had maintained with much heat that half the bloods behind the walls were put there by some vengeful bitch. Warriors for the revolution wasting away in the joint for nonsupport or some other domestic bullshit. "Well, that should point something out!" a sister in the rear had yelled, trying to be heard over a bunch of brothers who stood up to say big-mouth sisters like herself were responsible for Black misery.

Starving. Cliff had spaced on much of the discussion, thinking about his daughter Rhea. Going over in his mind what he might have said had he been there to hear Donna murmur, "Hey, Cliff, I think I missed my period." But he had been in the army. And later when the pregnancy was a certainty, he was in Norfolk, Virginia, on his way overseas, he thought. And all the way out of port he lay in his bunk, Donna's letter under his head, crinkly in the pillowcase, gassing with Carl Davis about that ever-breathtaking announcement that could wreck a perfectly fine relationship—Hey, baby, I think I'm pregnant.

He had not quite kept track of the workshop debate the night before, for he was thinking about parenthood, thinking too of his own parents, his mother ever on the move to someplace else his father'd been rumored to be but never was, dragging him and his little sister Alma all over the South till the relatives in Charlotte said whoa, sister, park em here. And he had grown up in a household of women only, women always. Crowded, fussed over, intruded upon, continually compared to and warned not to turn out like the dirty dog who'd abandoned Aunt Mavis or that no-good nigger who'd done Cousin Dorcas dirty or some other low-down bastard that didn't mean no woman no good.

"You're unusually preoccupied, Cliff," Aisha was saying gently, as if reluctant to intrude, but hesitant about leaving him alone to wrassle with the pain he was sure was readable in his face. "Not that I know you well enough to know what's usual." He followed her gaze toward the park. "You feel like walking a while? Talking? Or maybe just being quiet?"

"Thought you were starving?" He heard an edge to his voice, but she didn't seem to notice.

"I am. I am." She waited at the curb, ready to cross over to the park or straight ahead to the Indian restaurant. Cliff disengaged his arm and fished out a cigarette, letting the light change. Had he been alone, he would have crossed over to the park. He had put off taking inventory for too long, his life was in a drift, unmonitored. Just that morning shaving, trying to fix in his mind what role he'd been called on to play in the impending student takeover, he'd scanned the calendar over the sink. The student demands would hit the campus paper on the anniversary of the Bay of Pigs.

He'd made certain promises that day, that spring day in '61 when the boat shipped out for Vietnam they'd thought, but headed directly for the Caribbean. He'd made certain promises about what his life would be like in five years, ten years, ever after if he lived. Had made certain promises to himself, to the unborn child, to God, he couldn't remember to whom, as the ship of Puerto Ricans, Chicanos and Bloods were cold-bloodedly transported without their knowing from Norfolk to Cuba to kill for all the wrong reasons. Then the knowledge of where they were and what they were expected to do, reminded of the penalty for disobeying orders, he'd made promises through clenched teeth, not that he was any clearer about the Cuban Revolution than he was about the Vietnamese struggle, but he knew enough about Afro-Cuban music to make some connections and concluded that the secret mission was low-down. Knew too that if they died, no one at home'd be told the truth. Missing in action overseas. Taken by the Vietcong. Killed in Nam in the service of God and country.

"Worried?" Aisha asked, "or just reminiscing?"

He put his arm around her shoulders and hugged her close. His life was not at all the way he'd promised. "I was just thinking," he said slowly, crossing them toward the restaurant, "about the first time I came North as a kid." He wasn't sure that was a lie. The early days came crowding in on him every time he thought of his daughter and the future. And his daughter filled his mind on every mention of starving.

He hadn't even known as a boy that he was or for what, till that Sunday his aunts had hustled him and Alma to the train depot. But Granddaddy Mobley didn't even get off the train when it slowed. Just leaned down and hauled them up by the wrists, first Alma, then him.

"Hop aboard, son," he'd said, bouncing the cigar to the back of his jaw. "This what you call a rescue job."

Son. He had been sugar dumpling, sweetie pie, honey darling for so long, as though the horror of Southern living in general, the bitterness of being in particular some poor fatherless child could be sweetened with a sugar tit, and if large enough could fill him up, fill up those drafty places somewhere inside. So long hugged and honey-bunched, he didn't know he was starving or for what till "son" was offered him and the grip on his wrist became a handshake man to man.

Dumfounded, the women were trotting along after the still-moving train, Cousin Dorcas calling his name, Aunt Evelyn calling Granddaddy Mobley a bunch of names.

"Train, iz you crazy?" Aunt Mavis had demanded when she realized that was all the train intended to do, slow up for hopping off or kidnapping. "Have you lost your mind?" Cliff could never figure to whom this last remark was said. But he remembered he laughed like hell.

Granddaddy Mobley chuckled too, watching Cousin Dorcas through the gritty windows, trotting along the landing, shaking her fist, dodging the puffs of steam and the chunks of gravel thrown up by the wheels, the ribbons of her hat flying in and out of her shouting mouth.

Leaning out of an open window over his sister's head, Cliff could make out the women on the landing getting smaller, staring pop-eyed and pop-mouthed too. And when he glanced down, li'l Alma was looking straight up into his face the way she did from the bunk beds when the sun came up, the look asking was everything okay and could the day begin. He grinned back out the window, and grinned too at his sister cause yeah, everything would be all right. He couldn't blame the women, though, for carrying on like that, having taken all morning to get the chicken fried and the rugs swept and the sheets boiled and dough beat up. Then come to find old Mobley, highstepping, fun-loving, outrageous, drinking, rambler, gambler and everything else necessary to thoroughly scandalize the family name, upset the household with his annual visits, giving them something to talk about as the lamps glowed at night till next visiting time, old Mobley wasn't even thinking about a visit at all this time. Wasn't even stopping long enough to say hello to his daughter, not that she was there. Just came to snatch the darling little girl and the once perfect little gentleman now grown rusty and hardheaded just like his daddy for the world.

"We going North with you?" Alma had asked, not believing she could go anywhere without her flouncy dresses, her ribbons, and their mother's silver hairbrush from the world's fair.

"That's right."

"We going to live with you?" young Cliff had pressed, eager to get things straight. "To live with you till we grown or just for summer or what?"

Instead of answering, the old man whipped out a wad of large, white handkerchiefs and began to unfold them with very large gestures. The children settled in their seats waiting for the magic show to commence. But the old man just spread them out on the seats, three for sitting on and one for his hat. Cliff and Alma exchanged a look, lost for words. And in that moment, the old man leaned forward, snatched Alma's little yellow-haired doll and pitched it out the window.

"And you better not cry," he said.

"No, ma'am."

Cliff laughed and the old man frowned. "Unless you in training to take care of white folks' babies when you grown."

"No, ma'am."

Cliff had smiled smugly, certain that Alma had no idea what this rescue man was saying. He did. And he looked forward to growing up with a man like this. Alma slid her small hand into his and Cliff squeezed it. And not once did she look back after her doll, or he at the town.

"I met your wife in the bus terminal—"

"Ex-wife," Cliff said, jolted out of his reverie.

Aisha poured the tea. "Ex-wife. Met her last Monday and—"

"You told me."

"I didn't tell you the whole thing."

Cliff looked up from his plate of meat patties. He wasn't sure he wanted to hear about it. Every time he had tried to think of his daughter, he discovered he couldn't detach her from the woman he'd married. Thinking about Donna made him mad. Thinking about his daughter Rhea just made him breathless. Rising, he jingled change in his pocket and stalled for time at the jukebox. That was the first thing Aisha had said to him when they were introduced just four days ago on campus. "Hemphill? I think I know your wife, Donna Hemphill. Ran into her at the bus terminal less than an hour ago."

After his one class of the day and a quick meeting with the Black student union, he'd sought her out in the faculty dining room, convinced his chairman would at least give her the semi-deluxe treatment, particularly considering his taste for black meat (or so the rumor went, though he rarely did more toward orienting new faculty members than pointing out their cubicle, shoving a faculty handbook at them, and warning them about the "Mau Mau," his not-so-affectionate name for the Black student union). She had pursued the topic the minute Cliff had seated himself next to her, remarking quietly that his wife had seemed on the verge of collapse. He welcomed the mention of Donna only for the opportunity it offered to point out that one, she was very much an ex, two he was single, three he found her, Aisha, attractive. Beyond that, he could care less about Donna or her mental state. Aisha had remarked then—too sarcastically for his taste—that his very ex-wife with the mental state was the woman who was raising his daughter. He had eaten the dry roast beef sullenly, grateful for the appearance of his colleague Robinson, who swung the conversation toward the students and the massive coronaries they were causing in administrative circles.

Some Indian movie music blared out at Cliff's back as he picked out one of the umpteen rhythms to stroll back to the table doing, slapping out the beat on this thigh.

"I didn't say this before"—Aisha was reaching for the drumming hand—

"cause you cut me short last Tuesday. I'm sorry I didn't press it then on campus, cause it's harder now . . . that I know you . . . and all."

"Then forget it."

She slid her hand back to her side of the table and busied herself with the meat patties. He drummed on the table with both hands, trying to read her mood. He felt he owed her some explanation, wanted even to talk this thing out, his feelings about his daughter. Then resented Aisha for that. He drummed away. The last thing he would have wanted for this evening, the first time they'd been together with no other appointments to cut into their time, the last thing he wanted, feeling already a little off-center, crowded, was a return to that part of this history that seemed so other, over with, some dim drama starring a Cliff long since discarded. Cliff the soldier, Cliff the young father, Cliff the sociology instructor—there was clarity if not continuity. But Cliff the husband . . . blank.

He had pronounced the marriage null and void in the spring of '61. On the troop ship speeding to who knew where, or at least none of the dudes in that battalion knew yet, but to die most probably. He'd read the letter over and over, and was convinced Donna was lying about being pregnant and so far advanced. He was due home for good soon, and this was her way to have him postpone thinking of a split. He and Carl Davis had gassed the whole time out of port about what they were going to do with their lives if they still had them in five months' time. Then some of the soldiers were saying the fleet was in the Caribbean. And all hell broke loose, the men mistakenly assuming—assuming, then readying up for shore leave in Trinidad. The CO told them different, though not much. First there was a sheaf of papers that had to be signed, or court-martial, papers saying they never would divulge to press, to family, to friends, even to each other anything at all regarding the secret mission they were about to embark upon. Then they got their duties. Most work detail the same—painting over the ship's numbers, masking all U.S. identification, readying up the equipment for the gunners, checking their packs and getting new issues of ammunition.

"We're headed for Cuba," Carl Davis had said.

"That's crazy. The action's in Vietnam."

"Mate, I'm telling you, we're off to Cuba. T.J. was upside and got the word. The first invasionary battalions are Cuban exiles. They'll hook up with the forces there on the island to overthrow Fidel Castro."

"You got to be kidding."

Carl had sneered at Cliff's naivete. "Mate, they got air coverage that'd make the Luftwaffe look silly. We rendezvous with a carrier and a whole fleet of marines moving in from Nicaragua. I'm telling you, this is it."

T.J. had skidded down the stair rail and whispered. "They got Kennedy on a direct line. Kennedy! Jim, this operation is being directed from the top."

"Holy shit." Cliff had collapsed on his bunk, back pack and all, the letter crumpling under his ear. A child was being born soon, the letter said. He was going to be a father. And if he died, what would happen to his child? His marriage had been in shreds before he'd left, a mere patchwork job on the last leave, and she'd been talking of going back home. His child. Her parents. That world. Those people.

"I never knew Donna well," Aisha was saying. "We worked at Family Services and I used to see her around, jazz concerts, the clubs. I pretty much wrote her off as a type. One of those gray girls who liked to follow behind Black musicians, hang out and act funky."

Cliff looked at Aisha quickly. Was she the type to go for blood? He'd had enough of the white girl–brother thing. Had been sick of it all, of hearing, of reading about it, of arguing, of defending himself, even back then on the tail end of the Bohemian era, much less in the Black and Proud times since.

"Use to run into her a lot when I lived downtown. The baby didn't surprise me—hell, half of Chelsea traffic was white girls pushing mulatto babies in strollers. We used to chat. You two seemed to be always on the verge of breakup, and she was forever going down in flames. I got the impression the baby was something of . . . a hostage?" She seemed to wait for his response. He blanked his face out. "A hostage," she continued, seeming to relish the word, "as per usual."

The waiter slid a dish of chutney at Cliff's elbow, then leaned in to replace the teapot with a larger, steamier one. Cliff leaned back as the plates and bowls were taken from the tray in some definite, mysterious order and placed just so on the table. Cliff rearranged the plate of roti and the cabbage. The waiter looked at him and placed them in their original spots. Cliff sneaked a look at Aisha and they shared a stone-faced grin.

"Cliff?" She seemed to call to him, the him behind his poker face. He leaned forward. Whatever she had to say, it'd be over with soon and they could get on with the Friday evening he had in mind.

"I asked Donna on Tuesday to give up the child. To give your daughter to me. I'm prepared to raise—"

Cliff stared, not sure he heard that right.

"Look. She's standing in the bus terminal having a crying jag, listing fifty-leven different brands of humiliations and bump-offs from the Black community. She's been trying to enroll your daughter in an independent Black school, at a Yoruba cultural center, at the Bedford-Stuyvesant—"

"Bedford-Stuyvesant?"

"Yea, your wife lives in Brooklyn."

"Ex-wife."

Aisha spread her napkin and asked very pointedly, "You were not aware that your daughter's been living in Brooklyn for two years?" Cliff tried to remember the last address he had sent money to, recalled he had always given it to Alma.

But then Alma had moved to the coast last spring . . .

"Hey, look, Cliff, I've noticed the way you keep leaning on this ‛ex' business. I'm sure you're sick to death of people jumping on you, especially sisters, about the white-woman thing. Quite frankly, I don't give a shit who you married or who you are . . . not now . . . I only thought I did," she said, spacing her words out in a deliberate challenge. "What does interest me is the kid. I'll tell you just what I told her, I'm prepared to take the girl—"

"Hold it. Hold it." Cliff shoved his plate away and tried to sort out what he was hearing. If only he could have a tape of this, he was thinking, to play at his leisure, not have to respond or be read. "Back up, you're moving too fast for me. I'm just a country boy." He smiled, not surprised that she did smile back. She looked tired.

"Okay. She's been trying to move your daughter into cultural activities and whatnot. Very concerned about the kid's racial identity. For years she's always been asking me to suggest places to take her and how to handle things and so forth. So I'm standing in the bus terminal while this white woman falls apart on me, asking to be forgiven her incompetence, her racism, her hysteria. And I'm pissed. So I ask her—"

"Where's the nigger daddy who should be taking the weight."

Aisha studied her fork and resumed eating. Cliff clenched his jaws. She was eating now as though she'd been concentrating on that chicken curry for hours, had not even spoken, did not even know he was there. Was that the point of it all, to trigger that outburst? And it had been an outburst, his face was still burning. Was she out for blood? It was a drag. Cliff reached for the chutney and sensed her tense up. She looked coiled on her side of the table, mouth full of poisonous fangs. She was a type, he decided, a type he didn't like. She had seemed a groovy woman, but she was just another bitch. She had looked good to him less than half an hour ago, bouncing around in the white space shoes. Had looked good in that slippery white uniform wrinkling at her hips. And all he thought he wanted to do was take her to his place and tell her so, show her. He thought he still might like to take her home to make love to her—no, to fuck her. The atmosphere kept changing, the tone, the whole quality of his feelings for her kept shifting. She kept him off balance. Yeh, he'd like to fuck her, but not cause she looked good. Cliff tore off a piece of roti, then decided he didn't want it. Looked at her and decided he was being absurd. What had she said she was pissed about? Donna, an unhinged white woman raising a Black child. Why had he been so defensive?

"This was a bad time to meet," he heard himself saying. "I wish we had met at some other time when—"

"Look sugar," she spat out with a malice that didn't match the words, "no matter when or where or how we met, the father questions would've come up. And I'd have had to judge what kind of man you are behind your whole sense of what it means to bring a child into the world. I'm funny that way, mister."

"What I was thinking was," he pressed on, shoving aside the anger brewing, clamping down hard on the urge to bust her in the jaw, not sure the urge to hold her close wasn't just as strong, "in a year or so you might have met me with my daughter. I've been considering for a long time fighting for custody of Rhea."

"How long?"

"Off and on for years. But here lately, last few weeks . . ." It occurred to him that that was exactly what he'd been trying to pull together in his mind, a plan. That was what had been crowding him.

"Donna said she'd talk to you about it, Cliff, then get back to me. It was a serious proposal I was making."

"She hasn't called me. Matter of fact, we haven't talked in years."

"Uh-hunh." She delivered this with the jauntiness of a gum-cracking sister from Lenox Avenue. Cliff read on her face total disbelief of all he'd said, as though he couldn't have been really considering it and not talk with the child's mother. He was pissed off. How did it get to be her business, any of it?

"Anyway, Brother," she said, shifting into still another tone, "I'm prepared to take the child. I've got this job at the clinic, it'll hold me till summer when the teaching thing comes through. My aunt runs a school up on Edgecombe. She's not the most progressive sister in the world, but the curriculum's strong academically. And there're several couples on my block who get together and take the kids around. I'm good with children. Raised my nephews and my sisters. I'd do right by the little girl, Cliff. What do you want to ask me?"

Her voice had faded away to a whisper. She sipped her tea now, and for a minute he thought she was about to cry. He wasn't sure for what, but felt he was being unjustly blamed for something. She hadn't believed him. That made him feel unsure about himself. He watched her, drifting in and out among the fragments of sensations, questions that wouldn't stay formed long enough for him to get a hold of. He studied her until his food got cold.

She wasn't going to sleep with him, that was clear. He knew from past experiences that the moment had passed, that moment when women resolved the tension by deciding yes they would, then relaxed one way, or no they wouldn't, and eased into another rhythm. Often at the critical point, especially with younger women, he'd step into their timing and with one remark or a caress of the neck could turn the moment in his favor. He hadn't even considered it with Aisha. There had seemed time enough to move leisurely, no rush. They'd had dinner that first night, then he'd had a Black faculty meeting. He'd picked her up last night to get to the workshop, and after they'd had coffee with Acoli and Essa and talked way into the night about the students' demands. He hadn't even considered that this evening, which just a half-hour ago seem stretched out so casual and unrushed, would turn out as anything but right.

Hell, they weren't children. They had established right from the jump that this would be a relationship, a relationship of meaning. And he'd looked forward to it, had even thought of calling Alma long distance and working Aisha somehow into the conversation. He knew it would please his sister, for he knew well how it pained her whenever he launched into his dissertation on Black women, the bitterness for those Black women who had raised him surfacing always, and for the others so much like them—though Alma argued it wasn't so—who'd stepped into his life with such explosions, leaving ashes in their wake. And Alma argued that wasn't so either, just his own blindness contracted from poisons he should have pumped out somehow long ago cause they weren't reasonably come by either. He was sick of his dissertation, the arguing, the venom, even thinking about it.

"You can imagine, Cliff . . . well, the irony of it all, meeting you right after seeing Donna after all these years of running into her, hearing about you . . . Look, it's very complicated—my feelings about . . . the whole thing."

"How so?" He poured the last of the hot tea into her cup and waited. She seemed to study the cup for a long time as though considering whether to reject it, wait for it to cool, drink it, or maybe fling it in his face. He couldn't imagine why that last seemed such a possibility. His sister Alma would have argued that he simply expected the worst always and usually got it, provoked it.

"On the one hand, I'm very attracted to you, Cliff. You care about the students. I mean . . . well, you have a reputation on campus for being—" She was blushing and that surprised the hell out of him. He decided he didn't know women at all. They were too weird, all of them. "Well, for being one of the good guys. Plus you so sharp, ya know, and a great sense of humor. Not to mention you fine." She was looking suddenly girlish. He wanted to laugh, but he didn't want to interrupt her. He was liking this. "And I dig being with you. You're comfortable, even when you're drifting off, you're comfortable to be with." He bowed in his seat. They were smiling again.

"On the other hand"—she cocked her head to signal she hoped to get through this part with the same chumminess—"Well . . ." She drank the tea now, two fingers pressed on each side of the Oriental cup, her face moving into the steam, lips pursing to blow. If they ever got around to the pillow talk, he'd ask her about her gesture and whether or not it had been designed to get him. He found all this blowing and sipping very arousing, for no reason he could think of.

"On the other hand," she said again, "while you seem to be a principled person . . . I mean, clearly you're not a bastard or a coward . . . not handling the shit on campus like you been doing . . . but—" She put the cup down.

"Hey look. It's like this, Cliff. I don't understand brothers who marry white girls, I really don't. And I really don't see how you can just walk away from the kid, let your child just . . . Well, damn, what is your daughter, a souvenir?" It was clear to Cliff that his reaction was undisguised and that she was having no trouble reading his face. "Perhaps"—she was looking hopeful now, his cue to rise to the occasion—"perhaps you really have been trying to figure out how to do it, how to get custody?"

"I considered it long before we even broke up. When I first heard that the child was an actual fact, was about to be born, I was in the army. As a matter of fact, I was up to my neck in the Bay of Pigs shit." He had never discussed it before, was amazed he could do it now, could relate it all in five or six quick sentences, when times earlier he hadn't even been able to pull it together coherently in a whole night, staring at the ceiling, wondering how many brothers had been rerouted to the Philippines to put down the resistance to Marcos and the corporate bosses, how many to Ethiopia to vamp on the Eritrean Front, and how many would wind up in southern Africa all too soon, thinking they were going who knew where. How many more caught in the trick bag of colored on colored death if all who knew remained silent on the score, chumps afraid of change?

Cliff had always maintained he despised people who saw and heard but would not move on what they knew. His colleagues who could wax lyric analyzing the hidden agenda of SEEK and other OEO circuses engineered to fail, but did nothing about it. Bloods in his department grooming the students for caretaker positions, all the while screaming on the system, the oppression, hawking revolution, but carefully cultivating caretakers to negotiate a separate peace for a separate piece of the corrupt pie, claiming the next generation would surely do it. And even Cousin Dorcas and Aunt Mavis years before, going through a pan of biscuits and a pot of coffee laying out with crystal clarity the madness of his mother's life, chronically on hold till she could just get to that one more place to find the man never where folks said he'd be. But never once wrassling the woman, their sister, their kin, to the floor, demanding she at least put the children on her agenda, if not herself. And Cliff himself, heroic in spots, impotent in others, he had postponed for too long an inventory of his self, his life.

"The Cuban people were ready. They kicked our ass. That first landing troop ran smack into an alligator farm in Playa Giron and got wiped out. The second got wasted fore they even got off the beach. And all the while our ship was getting hit. And Kennedy on the line saying, 'Pull back,' realizing them balls were a warning, a reminder of what could happen in the world if the U.S. persisted."

Aisha poured him a glass of ginger beer and waited for him to continue. Cliff felt opened up like he hadn't been in years.

"The idea that I might be killed, that my wife Donna would move back to her parents, my child growing up in an all-white environment . . . I use to run the my-wife-is-an-individual-white-person number . . . I dunno . . . it all scared the shit out of me," he was saying, not able to find the bridge, the connection, the transition from those thoughts, those promises made in Cuban waters and what in fact he lived out later and called his life.

"When we broke up, I turned my back, I guess," he said, finding his place again, but not the bridge. "I use to see my daughter a lot when my sister Alma lived in the city. And if I could just figure out how to manage it all, have time for my work and—"

"Your work?" she said, clutching the tablecloth. "Your work?" she sneered. "You one of those dudes who thinks his 'real' work is always outside of—separate from—oh, shit."

He felt her withdraw. He would make an effort to draw her out again, even if she came out blazing in a hot tirade about "someone's work" and "men's work" and "what a load of horseshit." He would do it for himself. Later for the them that might have been.

"We were discussing all this recently in class—'The Black Family in the Twentieth Century,' my new course."

"Yeah, I know," she said.

"You know?"

"My niece is in your class. She tapes your lectures. Big fan of yours, my niece."

"Oh." Cliff couldn't remember now just what he had wanted to say, had lost the thread. Aisha had motioned the waiter and was scanning the dessert list. He shook his head. Dessert was not what he wanted at this point.

He had handed back the students' research papers on their own families when the vet who sat in the back got up to say how odd it was that their generation, meaning the sophomores or juniors, despite the persistent tradition in their own families of folks raising children not their own, odd that this younger generation felt exempt. How many here, someone in the front of the room had asked then, can see themselves adopting children or taking in a kid from the streets, or from a strung-out neighbor, as their own? Cliff had expected a split down the middle, the brothers opting for pure lineage, the sisters charging ego and making a case for "the children" rather than "my child." But it didn't go down that way. The discussion never got off the ground. And after class, the vet had criticized Cliff for short-circuiting the discussion. Cliff hadn't seen his point then. But now, watching Aisha coax the recipe for some dessert or other from the waiter, he could admit that he had probably spaced.

Naturally he'd been thinking of his daughter Rhea, wondering how many others in the class had children and whether it would be fruitful to ask that first. The problem was, he could never think of Rhea without also thinking of Donna. Even after he refused to visit the child on his wife's turf, preferring the serenity of Alma's home for the visits, Rhea was still daughter to the woman who'd been his wife. And he was outside.

He'd been so proud when as a baby she had learned to say "Daddy" first. That had knocked him out. His sister had offered some psycholinguistic-somethinorother explanation, completely unsolicited and halfway unheard, about a baby's physical capacity to produce *d* sounds long before *m* sounds. Cliff paid Alma no mind.

But as the baby grew more independent, more exploratory of the world beyond her skin, he realized why she could say "Daddy" so much sooner. Cause Mommy was not separate, Mommy was part of the baby's world, attached to her own ego. He was distinctly different. Outside. It was some time before Mommy was seen as other. And still later that Rhea could step back from herself and manage "Rhea," then "me." Meanwhile he was outside. Way before that even he was outside—pregnancy, labor, delivery, breastfeeding. Women and babies, mothers and children, mother and child. Him outside. If only she had looked more like him, though in fact she resembled Alma more than Donna. But still there was distance. He knew no terms for negotiating a relationship with her that did not also include her mother. How had Donna managed that? Hostage, Aisha had said.

He chuckled to himself and stared at Aisha. He started up a nutty film in his head. All over the country, sisters crouching behind bushes with croaker sacks ready to pounce and spirit away little mulatto babies. Mulatto babies were dearer, prizer. Or sisters shouting from the podiums, the rooftops, the bedrooms, telling warriors dirty diapers was revolutionary work. Sisters coiled in red leather booths mesmerizing fathers into a package deal. He clamped down hard on fantasies leaching poisons into his brain. Package dream—me and the kid.

"Were you proposing to me by any chance?" he asked just for the hell of it.

"Say what?" She first looked bewildered, then angry, then amazed. She burst out laughing, catching him off-guard when she asked in icy tones, "Is that basically your attitude? Big joke?"

He shrugged in innocence and decided to leave it alone. She was bristly. Let her eat her pastry and drink her mint tea, he instructed himself. Put her in a cab and send her home. He wanted time to himself, time to take a good look at the yellow chair Alma had bequeathed to him when she moved to the coast. Its unfolding capacity never failed to amaze him. It would make a better bed than the Disney pen he'd spied in a children's store that morning. He was feeling good again.

He leaned forward and Aisha slid a forkful of crumbly pastry into his mouth. She was looking good to him once more. He grinned. She jerked her chin as if to ask what was he about to say. He wasn't about to say anything. But he was thinking that no, they hadn't met at the wrong time. It'd been the right time for him. The wrong time for them maybe. But what the hell.

"What did you want to be when you grew up?" she asked. He leaned in for another forkful of pastry. "Just don't be like your daddy" rang in his ears. "A tender man," he said and watched her lashes flutter lower.

The question he would put to himself when he got home and stretched out in that yellow chair was what had he promised his daughter in the spring of '61. He smiled at Aisha and leaned up out of his chair to kiss her on the forehead. She blushed. He was sure he could come true for the Cliff he'd been.

PARKER'S BACK

Flannery O'Connor

Parker's wife was sitting on the front porch floor, snapping beans. Parker was sitting on the step, some distance away, watching her sullenly. She was plain, plain. The skin on her face was thin and drawn as tight as the skin on an onion and her eyes were grey and sharp like the points of two icepicks. Parker understood why he had married her—he couldn't have got her any other way—but he couldn't understand why he stayed with her now. She was pregnant and pregnant women were not his favorite kind. Nevertheless, he stayed as if she had him conjured. He was puzzled and ashamed of himself.

The house.they rented sat alone save for a single tall pecan tree on a high embankment overlooking a highway. At intervals a car would shoot past below and his wife's eyes would swerve suspiciously after the sound of it and then come back to rest on the newspaper full of beans in her lap. One of the things she did not approve of was automobiles. In addition to her other bad qualities, she was forever sniffing up sin. She did not smoke or dip, drink whiskey, use bad language or paint her face, and God knew some paint would have improved it, Parker thought. Her being against color, it was the more remarkable she had married him. Sometimes he supposed that she had married him because she meant to save him. At other times he had a suspicion that she actually liked everything she said she didn't. He could account for her one way or another, it was himself he could not understand.

She turned her head in his direction and said, "It's no reason you can't work for a man. It don't have to be a woman."

"Aw shut your mouth for a change," Parker muttered.

If he had been certain she was jealous of the woman he worked for he would have been pleased but more likely she was concerned with the sin that would result if he and the woman took a liking to each other. He had told her that the woman was a hefty young blonde; in fact she was nearly seventy years old and too dried up to have an interest in anything except getting as much work out of him as she could. Not that an old woman didn't sometimes get an interest in a young man, particularly if he was as attractive as Parker felt he was, but this old woman looked at him the same way she looked at her old tractor—as if she had to put up with it because it was all she had. The tractor had broken down the second day Parker was on it and she had set him at once to cutting bushes, saying out of the side of her mouth to the nigger, "Everything he touches, he breaks." She also asked him to wear his shirt when he worked; Parker had removed it even though the day was not sultry; he put it back on reluctantly.

The ugly woman Parker married was his first wife. He had had other women but he had planned never to get himself tied up legally. He had first seen her one morning when his truck broke down on the highway. He had managed to pull it off the road into a neatly swept yard on which sat a peeling two-room house. He got out and opened the hood of the truck and began to study the motor. Parker had an extra sense that told him when there was a woman nearby watching him. After he had leaned over the motor a few minutes, his neck began to prickle. He cast his eye over the empty yard and porch of the house. A woman he could not see was either nearby beyond a clump of honeysuckle or in the house, watching him out the window.

Suddenly Parker began to jump up and down and fling his hand about as if he had smashed it in the machinery. He doubled over and held his hand close to his chest. "God dammit!" he hollered, "Jesus God Almighty damm! God dammit to hell!" he went on, flinging out the same few oaths over and over as loud as he could.

Without warning a terrible bristly claw slammed the side of his face and he fell backwards on the hood of the truck. "You don't talk no filth here!" a voice close to him shrilled.

Parker's vision was so blurred that for an instant he thought he had been attacked by some creature from above, a giant hawk-eyed angel wielding a hoary weapon. At his sight cleared, he saw before him a tall raw-boned girl with a broom.

"I hurt my hand," he said. "I HURT my hand." He was so incensed that he forgot that he hadn't hurt his hand. "My hand may be broke," he growled although his voice was still unsteady.

"Lemme see it," the girl demanded.

Parker stuck out his hand and she came closer and looked at it. There was not a mark on the palm and she took the hand and turned it over. His own hand was dry and hot and rough and Parker felt himself jolted back to life by her touch. He looked more closely at her. I don't want nothing to do with this one, he thought.

The girl's sharp eyes peered at the back of the stubby reddish hand he held. There emblazoned in red and blue was a tattooed eagle perched on a cannon. Parker's sleeve was rolled to the elbow. Above the eagle a serpent was coiled about a shield and in the spaces between the eagle and the serpent there were hearts, some with arrows through them. Above the serpent there was a spread hand of cards. Every space on the skin of Parker's arm, from wrists to elbow, was covered in some loud design. The girl gazed at this with an almost stupefied smile of shock, as if she had accidentally grasped a poisonous snake; she dropped the hand.

"I got most of my other ones in foreign parts," Parker said. "These here I mostly got in the United States. I got my first one when I was only fifteen years old."

"Don't tell me," the girl said, "I don't like it. I ain't got any use for it."

"You ought to see the ones you can't see," Parker said and winked.

Two circles of red appeared like apples on the girl's cheeks and softened her appearance. Parker was intrigued. He did not for a minute think that she didn't like the tattoos. He had never yet met a woman who was not attracted to them.

Parker was fourteen when he saw a man in a fair, tattooed from head to foot. Except for his loins which were girded with a panther hide, the man's skin was patterned in what seemed from Parker's distance—he was near the back of the tent, standing on a bench—a single intricate design of brilliant color. The man, who was small and sturdy, moved about on the platform, flexing his muscles so that the arabesque of man and beasts and flowers on his skin appeared to have a subtle motion of its own. Parker was filled with emotion, lifted up as some people are when the flag passes. He was a boy whose mouth habitually hung open. He was heavy and earnest, as ordinary as a loaf of bread. When the show was over, he had remained standing on the bench, staring where the tattooed man had been until the tent was almost empty.

Parker had never before felt the least notion of wonder in himself. Until he saw the man at the fair, it did not enter his head that there was anything out of the ordinary about the fact that he existed. Even then it did not enter his head, but a peculiar unease settled in him. It was as if a blind boy had been turned so gently in a different direction that he did not know his destination had been changed.

He had his first tattoo some time after—the eagle perched on the cannon. It was done by a local artist. It hurt very little, just enough to make it appear to Parker to be worth doing. This was peculiar too for before he had thought that only what did not hurt was worth doing. The next year he quit school because he was sixteen and could. He went to the trade school for a while, then he quit the trade school and worked for six months in a garage. The only reason he worked at all was to pay for more tattoos. His mother worked in a laundry and could support him, but she would not pay for any tattoo except her name on a heart, which he had put on, grumbling. However, her name was Betty Jean and nobody had to know it was his mother. He found out that the tattoos were attractive to the kind of girls he liked but who had never liked him before. He began to drink beer and get in fights. His mother wept over what was becoming of him. One night she dragged him off to a revival with her, not telling him where they were going. When he saw the big lighted church, he jerked out of her grasp and ran. The next day he lied about his age and joined the navy.

Parker was large for the tight sailor's pants but the silly white cap, sitting low on his forehead, made his face by contrast look thoughtful and almost intense. After a month or two in the navy, his mouth ceased to hang open. His features hardened into the features of a man. He stayed in the navy five years and seemed a natural part of the grey mechanical ship, except for his eyes, which were the same pale slate-color as the ocean and reflected the immense spaces around him as if they were a microcosm of the mysterious sea. In port Parker wandered about comparing the run-down places he was in to Birmingham, Alabama.

Everywhere he went he picked up more tattoos.

He had stopped having lifeless ones like anchors and crossed rifles. He had a tiger and a panther on each shoulder, a cobra coiled about a torch on his chest, hawks on his thighs, Elizabeth II and Philip over where his stomach and liver were respectively. He did not care much what the subject was so long as it was colorful; on his abdomen he had a few obscenities but only because that seemed the proper place for them. Parker would be satisfied with each tattoo about a month, then something about it that attracted him would wear off. Whenever a decent-sized mirror was available, he would get in front of it and study his overall look. The effect was not of one intricate arabesque of colors but of something haphazard and botched. A huge dissatisfaction would come over him and he would go off and find another tattooist and have another space filled up. The front of Parker was almost completely covered but there were no tattoos on his back. He had no desire for one anywhere he could not readily see it himself. As the space on the front of him for tattoos decreased, his dissatisfaction grew and became general.

After one of his furloughs, he didn't go back to the navy but remained away without official leave, drunk, in a rooming house in a city he did not know. His dissatisfaction, from being chronic and latent, had suddenly become acute and raged in him. It was as if the panther and the lion and the serpents and the eagles and the hawks had penetrated his skin and lived inside him in a raging warfare. The navy caught up with him, put him in the brig for nine months and gave him a dishonorable discharge.

After that Parker decided that country air was the only kind fit to breathe. He rented the shack on the embankment and bought the old truck and took various jobs which he kept as long as it suited him. At the time he met his future wife, he was buying apples by the bushel and selling them for the same price by the pound to isolated homesteaders on back country roads.

"All that there," the woman said, pointing to his arm, "is no better than what a fool Indian would do. It's a heap of vanity." She seemed to have found the word she wanted. "Vanity of vanities," she said.

Well what the hell do I care what she thinks of it? Parker asked himself, but he was plainly bewildered. "Reckon you like one of these better than another anyway," he said, dallying until he thought of something that would impress her. He thrust the arm back at her. "Which you like best?"

"None of them," she said, "but the chicken is not as bad as the rest."

"What chicken?" Parker almost yelled.

She pointed to the eagle.

"That's an eagle," Parker said. "What fool would waste their time having a chicken put on themself?"

"What fool would have any of it?" the girl said and turned away. She went slowly back to the house and left him there to get going. Parker remained for almost five minutes, looking agape at the dark door she had entered.

The next day he returned with a bushel of apples. He was not one to be outdone by anything that looked like her. He liked women with meat on them, so you didn't feel their muscles, much less their bone. When he arrived, she was sitting on the top step and the yard was full of children, all as thin and poor as herself; Parker remembered it was Saturday. He hated to be making up to a woman when there were children around, but it was fortunate he had brought the bushel of apples off the truck. As the children approached him to see what he carried, he gave each child an apple and told it to get lost; in that way he cleared out the whole crowd.

The girl did nothing to acknowledge his presence. He might have been a stray pig or goat that had wandered into the yard and she tried to take up the broom and sent it off. He set the bushel of apples down next to her on the step. He sat down on a lower step.

"Help yourself," he said, nodding at the basket; then he lapsed into silence.

She took an apple quickly as if the basket might disappear if she didn't make haste. Hungry people made Parker nervous. He had always had plenty to eat himself. He grew very uncomfortable. He reasoned he had nothing to say so why should he say it? He could not think now why he had come or why he didn't go before he wasted another bushel of apples on the crowd of children. He supposed they were her brothers and sisters.

She chewed the apple slowly but with a kind of relish of concentration, bent slightly but looking out ahead. The view from the porch stretched off across a long incline studded with iron weed and across the highway to a vast vista of hills and one small mountain. Long views depressed Parker. You look out into space like that and you begin to feel as if someone were after you, the navy or the government or religion.

"Who them children belong to, you?" he said at length.

"I ain't married yet," she said, "They belong to momma." She said it as if it were only a matter of time before she would be married.

Who in God's name would marry her? Parker thought.

A large barefooted woman with a wide gap-toothed face appeared in the door behind Parker. She had apparently been there for several minutes.

"Good evening," Parker said.

The woman crossed the porch and picked up what was left of the bushel of apples. "We thank you," she said and returned with it into the house.

"That your old woman?" Parker muttered.

The girl nodded. Parker knew a lot of sharp things he could have said like "You got my sympathy," but he was gloomily silent. He just sat there, looking at the view. He thought he must be coming down with something.

"If I pick up some peaches tomorrow I'll bring you some," he said.

"I'll be much obliged to you," the girl said.

Parker had no intention of taking any basket of peaches back there but the next day he found himself doing it. He and the girl had almost nothing to say to each other. One thing he did say was, "I ain't got any tattoo on my back."

"What you got on it?" the girl said politely.

"My shirt," Parker said. "Haw."

"Haw, haw," the girl said politely.

Parker thought he was losing his mind. He could not believe for a minute that he was attracted to a woman like this. She showed not the least interest in anything but what he brought until he appeared the third time with two cantaloupes. "What's your name?" she asked.

"O.E. Parker," he said.

"What does the O.E. stand for?"

"You can just call me O.E." Parker said. "Or Parker. Don't nobody call me by my name."

"What's it stand for?" she persisted.

"Never mind," Parker said. "What's yours?"

"I'll tell you when you tell me what them letters are the short of," she said. There was just a hint of flirtatiousness in her tone and it went rapidly to Parker's head. He had never revealed the name to any man or woman, only to the files of the navy and the government, and it was on his baptismal record which he got at the age of a month; his mother was a Methodist. When the name leaked out of the navy files, Parker narrowly missed killing the man who used it.

"You'll go blab it around," he said.

"I'll swear I'll never tell nobody," she said. "On God's holy work I swear it."

Parker sat for a few minutes in silence. Then he reached for the girl's neck, drew her ear close to his mouth and revealed the name in a low voice.

"Obadiah," she whispered. Her face slowly brightened as if the name came as a sign to her. "Obadiah," she said.

The name still stunk in Parker's estimation.

"Obadiah Elihue," she said in a reverent voice.

"If you call me that aloud, I'll bust your head open," Parker said. "What's yours?"

"Sarah Ruth Cates," she said.

"Glad to meet you, Sarah Ruth," Parker said.

Sarah Ruth's father was a Straight Gospel preacher but he was away, spreading it in Florida. Her mother did not seem to mind his attention to the girl so long as he brought a basket of something with him when he came. As for Sarah Ruth herself, it was plain to Parker after he had visited three times that she was crazy about him. She liked him even though she insisted that pictures on the skin were vanity of vanities and even after hearing him curse, and even after she had asked him if he was saved and he had replied that he didn't see it was anything in particular to save him from. After that, inspired, Parker had said, "I'd be saved enough if you was to kiss me."

She scowled. "That ain't being saved," she said.

Not long after that she agreed to take a ride in his truck. Parker parked it on a deserted road and suggested to her that they lie down together in the back of it.

"Not until after we're married," she said—just like that.

"Oh that ain't necessary," Parker said and as he reached for her, she thrust him away with such force that the door of the truck came off and he found himself flat on his back on the ground. He made up his mind then and there to have nothing further to do with her.

They were married in the County Ordinary's office because Sarah Ruth thought churches were idolatrous. Parker had no opinion about that one way or the other. The Ordinary's office was lined with cardboard file boxes and record books with dusty yellow slips of paper hanging on out of them. The Ordinary was an old woman with red hair who had held office for forty years and looked as dusty as her books. She married them from behind the iron-grill of a standup desk and when she finished, she said with a flourish, "Three dollars and fifty cents and till death do you part!" and yanked some forms out of a machine.

Marriage did not change Sarah Ruth a jot and it made Parker gloomier than ever. Every morning he decided he had had enough and would not return that night; every night he returned. Whenever Parker couldn't stand the way he felt, he would have another tattoo, but the only surface left on him now was his back. To see a tattoo on his own back he would have to get two mirrors and stand between them in just the correct position and this seemed to Parker a good way to make an idiot of himself. Sarah Ruth who, if she had had better sense, could have enjoyed a tattoo on his back, would not even look at the ones he had elsewhere. When he attempted to point out special details of them, she would shut her eyes tight and turn her back as well. Except in total darkness, she preferred Parker dressed and with his sleeves rolled down.

"At the judgment seat of God, Jesus is going to say to you, 'What you been doing all your life besides have pictures drawn all over you?'" she said.

"You don't fool me none," Parker said, "you're just afraid that hefty girl I work for'll like me so much she'll say, 'Come on, Mr. Parker, let's you and me . . .'"

"You're tempting sin," she said, "and at the judgment seat of God you'll have to answer for that too. You ought to go back to selling the fruits of the earth."

Parker did nothing much when he was at home but listen to what the judgment seat of God would be like for him if he didn't change his ways. When he could, he broke in with tales of the hefty girl he worked for. "'Mr. Parker,'" he said she said, 'I hired you for your brains.' (She had added, "So why don't you use them?")

"And you should have seen her face the first time she saw me without my shirt," he said. "'Mr. Parker,' she said, 'you're a walking panner-rammer!'" This had, in fact, been her remark but it had been delivered out of one side of her mouth.

Dissatisfaction began to grow so great in Parker that there was no containing it outside of a tattoo. It had to be his back. There was not help for it. A dim half-formed inspiration began to work in his mind. He visualized having a tattoo put there that Sarah Ruth would not be able to resist—a religious subject. He thought of an open book with HOLY BIBLE tattooed under it and an actual verse printed on the page. That seemed just the thing for a while; then he began to hear her say, "Ain't I already got a real Bible? What you think I want to read the same verse over and over for when I can read it all?" He needed something better even than the Bible! He thought about it so much that he began to lose sleep. He was already losing flesh—Sarah Ruth just threw food in the pot and let it boil. Not knowing for certain why he continued to stay with a woman who was both ugly and pregnant and could not cook made him generally nervous and irritable, and he developed a little tic in the side of his face.

Once or twice he found himself turning around abruptly as if someone was trailing him. He had had a granddaddy who had ended in the state mental hospital, although not until he was seventy-five, but as urgent as it might be for him to get a tattoo, it was just as urgent that he get exactly the right one to bring Sarah Ruth to heel. As he continued to worry over it, his eyes took on a hollow preoccupied expression. The old woman he worked for told him that if he couldn't keep his mind on what he was doing, she knew where she could find a fourteen-year-old colored boy who could. Parker was too preoccupied even to be offended. At any time previous, he would have left her then and there, saying dryly, "Well, you go ahead on and get him then."

Two or three mornings later he was baling hay with the old woman's sorry baler and her broken down tractor in a large field, cleared save for one enormous old tree standing in the middle of it. The old woman was the kind who would not cut down a large old tree because it was a large old tree. She had pointed it out to Parker as if he didn't have eyes and told him to be careful not to hit it as the machine picked up hay near it. Parker began at the outside of the field and made circles inward toward it. He had to get off the tractor every now and then and untangle the baling cord or kick a rock out of the way. The old woman had told him to carry the rocks to the edge of the field, which he did when she was there watching. When he thought he could make it, he ran over them. As he circled the field his mind was on a suitable design for his back. The sun, the size of a golf ball, began to switch regularly from in front to behind him, but he appeared to see it both places as if he had eyes in the back of his head. All at once he saw the tree reaching out to grasp him. A ferocious thud propelled him into the air, and he heard himself yelling in an unbelievable loud voice, "GOD ABOVE!"

He landed on his back while the tractor crashed upside-down into the tree and burst into flames. The first thing Parker saw were his shoes, quickly being eaten by the fire; one was caught under the tractor, the other was some distance away, burning by itself. He was not in them. He could feel the hot breath of the burning tree on his face. He scrambled backwards, still sitting, his eyes cavernous, and if he had known how to cross himself he would have done it.

His truck was on a dirt road at the edge of the field. He moved toward it, still sitting, still backwards, but faster and faster; halfway to it he got up and began a kind of forward-bent run from which he collapsed on his knees twice. His legs felt like two old rusted rain gutters. He reached the truck finally and took off in it, zigzagging up the road. He drove past his house on the embankment and straight for the city, fifty miles distant.

Parker did not allow himself to think on the way to the city. He only knew that there had been a great change in his life, a leap forward into a worse unknown, and that there was nothing he could do about it. It was for all intents accomplished.

The artist had two large cluttered rooms over a chiropodist's office on a back street. Parker, still barefooted, burst silently in on him at a little after three in the afternoon. The artist, who was about Parker's own age—twenty-eight—but thin and bald, was behind a small drawing table, tracing a design in green ink. He looked up with an annoyed glance and did not seem to recognize Parker in the hollow-eyed creature before him.

"Let me see the book you go with all the pictures of God in it," Parker said breathlessly. "The religious one."

The artist continued to look at him with his intellectual, superior stare. "I don't put tattoos on drunks," he said.

"You know me!" Parker cried indignantly. "I'm O.E. Parker! You done work for me before and I always paid!"

The artist looked at him another moment as if he were not altogether sure. "You've fallen off some," he said. "You must have been in jail."

"Married," Parker said.

"Oh," said the artist. With the aid of mirrors the artist had tattooed on top of his head a miniature owl, perfect in every detail. It was about the size of a half-dollar and served him as a show piece. There were cheaper artists in town but Parker had never wanted anything but the best. The artist went over to a cabinet at the back of the room and began to look over some art books. "Who are you interested in?" he said, "saints, angels, Christs or what?"

"God," Parker said.

"Father, Son or Spirit?"

"Just God," Parker said impatiently. "Christ. I don't care. Just so it's God."

The artist returned with a book. He moved some papers off another table and put the book down on it and told Parker to sit down and see what he liked. "The up-t-date ones are in the back," he said.

Parker sat down with the book and wet his thumb. He began to go through it, beginning at the back where the up-to-date pictures were. Some of them he recognized—The Good Shepherd, Forbid Them Not, The Smiling Jesus, Jesus the Physician's Friend, but he kept turning rapidly backwards and the pictures became less reassuring. One showed a gaunt green dead face streaked with blood.

One was yellow with sagging purple eyes. Parker's heart began to beat faster and faster until it appeared to be roaring inside him like a great generator. He flipped the pages quickly, feeling that when he reached the one ordained, a sign would come. He continued to flip through until he had almost reached the front of the book. On one of the pages a pair of eyes glanced at him swiftly. Parker sped on, then stopped. His heart too appeared to cut off; there was absolute silence. It said as plainly as if silence were a language itself, GO BACK.

Parker returned to the picture—the haloed head of a flat stern Byzantine Christ with all-demanding eyes. He sat there trembling; his heart began slowly to beat again as if it were being brought to life by a subtle power.

"You found what you want?" the artist asked.

Parker's throat was too dry to speak. He got up and thrust the book at the artist, opened at the picture.

"That'll cost you plenty," the artist said. "You don't want all those little blocks though, just the outline and some better features."

"Just like it is," Parker said, "just like it is or nothing."

"It's your funeral," the artist said, "but I don't do that kind of work for nothing."

"How much?" Parker asked.

"It'll take maybe two days work."

"How much?" Parker said.

"On time or cash?" the artist asked. Parker's other jobs had been on time, but he had paid.

"Ten down and ten for every day it takes," the artist said.

Parker drew ten dollar bills out of his wallet; he had three left in.

"You come back in the morning," the artist said, putting the money in his own pocket. "First I'll have to trace that out of the book."

"No, no!" Parker said. "Trace it now or gimme my money back," and his eyes glared as if he were ready for a fight.

The artist agreed. Anyone stupid enough to want a Christ on his back, he reasoned, would be just as likely as not to change his mind the next minute, but once the work was begun he could hardly do so.

While he worked on tracing, he told Parker to go wash his back at the sink with the special soap he used there. Parker did it and returned to pace back and forth across the room, nervously flexing his shoulders. He wanted to go look at the picture again but at the same time he did not want to. The artist got up finally and had Parker lie down on the table. He swabbed his back with ethyl chloride and then began to outline the head on it with his iodine pencil. Another hour passed before he took up his instrument. Parker felt no particular pain. In Japan he had had a tattoo of Buddha done on his upper arm with ivory needles; in Burma, a little brown root of a man had made a peacock on each of his knees using thin pointed sticks, two feet long, amateurs had worked on him with pins and soot. Parker was usually so relaxed and easy under the hand of the artist that he often went to sleep, but this time he remained awake, every muscle taut.

At midnight the artist said he was ready to quit. He propped one mirror, four feet square, on a table by the wall and took a smaller mirror off the lavatory wall and put it in Parker's hands. Parker stood with his back to the one on the table and moved the other until he saw a flashing burst of color reflected from his back. It was almost completely covered with little red and blue and ivory and saffron squares; from them he made out the lineaments of the face—a mouth, the beginning of heavy brows, a straight nose, but the face was empty; the eyes had not yet been put in. The impression for the moment was almost as if the artist had tricked him and done the Physician's Friend.

"It don't have eyes," Parker cried out.

"That'll come," the artist said, "in due time. We have another day to go on it yet."

Parker spent the night on a cot at the Haven of Light Christian Mission. He found these the best places to stay in the city because they were free and included a meal of sorts. He got the last available cot and because he was still barefooted, he accepted a pair of second-hand shoes which, in his confusion, he put on to go to bed; he was still shocked from all that had happened to him. All night he lay awake in the long dormitory of cots with lumpy figures on them. The only light was from a phosphorescent cross glowing at the end of the room. The tree reached out to grasp him again, then burst into flame; the shoe burned quietly by itself; the eyes in the book said to him distinctly GO BACK and at the same time did not utter a sound. He wished that he were not in this city, not in this Haven of Light Mission, not in a bed by himself. He longed miserably for Sarah Ruth. He decided he was losing it. His eyes appeared soft and dilatory compared with the eyes in the book, for even though he could not summon up the exact look of those eyes, he could still feel their penetration. He felt as though, under their gaze, he was as transparent as the wing of a fly.

The tattooist had told him not to come until ten in the morning, but when he arrived at that hour, Parker was sitting in the dark hallway on the floor, waiting for him. He had decided upon getting up that, once the tattoo was on him, he would not look at it, that all his sensations of the day and night before were those of a crazy man and that he would return to doing things according to his own sound judgement.

The artist began where he left off. "One thing I want to know," he said presently as he worked over Parker's back, "why do you want this on you? Have you gone and got religion? Are you saved?" he asked in a mocking voice.

Parker's throat felt salty and dry. "Naw," he said, "I ain't got no use for none of that. A man can't save his self from whatever it is he don't deserve none of my sympathy." These words seemed to leave his mouth like wraiths and to evaporate at once as if he had never uttered them.

"Then why . . ."

"I married this woman that's saved," Parker said. "I never should have done it. I ought to leave her. She's done gone and got pregnant."

"That's too bad," the artist said. "Then it's her making you have this tattoo."

"Naw," Parker said, "she don't know nothing about it. It's a surprise for her."

"You think she'll like it and lay off you a while?"

"She can't help herself," Parker said. "She can't say she don't like the looks of God." He decided he had told the artist enough of his business. Artists were all right in their place but he didn't like them poking their noses into the affairs of regular people. "I didn't get no sleep last night," he said. "I think I'll get some now."

That closed the mouth of the artist but it did not bring him any sleep. He lay there, imagining how Sarah Ruth would be struck speechless by the face on his back and every now and then this would be interrupted by a vision of the tree of fire and his empty shoe burning beneath it.

The artist worked steadily until nearly four o'clock, not stopping to have lunch, hardly pausing with the electric instrument except to wipe the dripping dye off Parker's back as he went along. Finally he finished. "You can get up and look at it now," he said.

Parker sat up but he remained on the edge of the table.

The artist was pleased with his work and wanted Parker to look at it at once. Instead Parker continued to sit on the edge of the table, bent forward slightly with a vacant look.

"What ails you?" the artist said. "Go look at it."

"Ain't nothing ail me," Parker said in a sudden belligerent voice. "That tattoo ain't going nowhere. It'll be there when I get there." He reached for his shirt and began gingerly to put it on.

The artist took him roughly by the arm and propelled him between the two mirrors. "Now look," he said, angry at having his work ignored.

Parker looked, turned white and moved away. The eyes in the reflected face continued to look at him—still, straight, all-demanding, enclosed in silence.

"It was your idea, remember," the artist said. "I would have advised something else."

Parker said nothing. He put on his shirt and went out the door while the artist shouted, "I'll expect all of my money!"

Parker headed toward a package shop on the corner. He bought a pint of whiskey and took it into a nearby alley and drank it all in five minutes. Then he moved on to a pool hall nearby which he frequented when he came to the city. It was a well-lighted barn-like place with a bar up one side and gambling machines on the other and pool tables in the back. As soon as Parker entered, a large man in a red and black checkered shirt hailed him by slapping him on the back yelling, "Yeyyyyyy boy! O.E. Parker!"

Parker was not yet ready to be struck on the back. "Lay off," he said, "I got a fresh tattoo there."

"What you got this time?" the man asked and then yelled to a few at the machines. "O.E.'s got him another tattoo."

"Nothing special this time," Parker said and slunk over to machine that was not being used.

"Come on," the big man said, "let's have a look at O.E.'s tattoo," and while Parker squirmed in their hands, they pulled up his shirt. Parker felt all the hands drop away instantly and his shirt fell again like a veil over the face. There was a silence in the pool room which seemed to Parker to grow from the circle around him until it extended to the foundations under the building and upward through the beams in the roof.

Finally someone said, "Christ!" Then they all broke into noise at once. Parker turned around, an uncertain grin on his face.

"Leave it to O.E.!" the man in the checkered shirt said. "That boy's a real card!"

"Maybe he's gone and got religion," someone yelled.

"Not on your life," Parker said.

"O.E.'s got religion and is witnessing for Jesus, ain't you, O.E.!" a little man with a piece of cigar in his mouth said wryly. "An o-riginal way to do it if I ever saw one."

"Leave it to Parker to think of a new one!" the fat man said.

"Yyeeeeeeyyyyyy boy!" someone yelled and they all began to whistle and curse in compliment until Parker said, "Aaa shut up."

"What'd you do it for?" somebody asked.

"For laughs," Parker said. "What's it to you?"

"Why ain't you laughing then?" somebody yelled. Parker lunged into the midst of them and like a whirlwind on a summer's day there began a fight that raged amid overturned tables and swinging fists until two of them grabbed him and ran to the door with him and threw him out. Then a calm descended on the pool hall as nerve shattering as if the long barn-like room were the ship from which Jonah had been cast into the sea.

Parker sat for a long time on the ground in the alley behind the pool hall, examining his soul. He saw it as a spider web of facts and lies that was not at all important to him but which appeared to be necessary in spite of his opinion. The eyes that were now forever on his back were eyes to be obeyed. He was as certain of it as he had ever been of anything. Throughout his life, grumbling and sometimes cursing, often afraid, once in rapture, Parker had obeyed whatever instinct of this kind had come to him—in rapture when his spirit had lifted at the sight of the tattooed man at the fair, afraid when he had joined the navy, grumbling when he had married Sarah Ruth.

The thought of her brought him slowly to his feet. She would know what he had to do. She would clear up the rest of it, and she would at least be pleased. It seemed to him that, all along, that was what he wanted, to please her. His truck was still parked in front of the building where the artist had his place, but it was not far away. He got in it and drove out of the city and into the country night. His head was almost clear of liquor and he observed that his dissatisfaction was gone, but he felt not quite like himself. It was as if he were himself but a stranger to himself, driving into a new country though everything he saw was familiar to him, even at night.

He arrived finally at the house on the embankment, pulled the truck under the pecan tree and got out. He made as much noise as possible to assert that he was still in charge here, that his leaving her for a night without word meant nothing except it was the way he did things. He slammed the car door, stamped up the two steps and across the porch and rattled the door knob. It did not respond to his touch. "Sarah Ruth!" he yelled, "let me in."

There was no lock on the door and she had evidently placed the back of a chair against the knob. He began to beat on the door and rattle the knob at the same time.

He heard the bed springs creak and bent down and put his head to the keyhole, but it was stopped up with paper. "Let me in!" he hollered, bamming the door again. "What you got me locked out for?"

A sharp voice close to the door said, "Who's there?"

"Me," Parker said, "O.E."

Still no sound from inside.

He tried once more. "O.E.," he said bamming the door two or three more times. "O.E. Parker. You know me."

There was a silence. Then the voice said slowly, "I don't know no O.E."

"Quit fooling," Parker pleaded. "You ain't got any business doing me this way. It's me, old O.E., I'm back. You ain't afraid of me."

"Who's there?" the same unfeeling voice said.

Parker turned his head as if he expected someone behind him to give him the answer. The sky had lightened slightly and there were two or three streaks of yellow floating above the horizon. Then as he stood there, a tree of light burst over the skyline.

Parker fell back against the door as if he had been pinned there by a lance.

"Who's there?" the voice from inside said and there was a quality about it now that seemed final. The knob rattled and the voice said peremptorily, "Who's there, I ast you?"

Parker bent down and put his mouth near the stuffed keyhole. "Obadiah," he whispered and all at once he felt the light pouring through him, turning his spider web soul into a perfect arabesque of colors, a garden of trees and birds and beasts.

"Obadiah Elihue!" he whispered.

The door opened and he stumbled in. Sarah Ruth loomed there, hands on her hips. She began at once, "That hefty blonde woman you was working for said you'll have to pay her every penny on her tractor you busted up. She don't keep insurance on it. She came here and her and me had us a long talk and I . . ."

Trembling, Parker set about lighting the kerosene lamp.

"What's the matter with you, wasting that keresene this near daylight?" she demanded. "I ain't got to look at you."

A yellow glow enveloped them. Parker put the match down and began to unbutton his shirt.

"And you ain't going to have none of me this near morning," she said.

"Shut your mouth," he said quietly. "Look at this and then I don't want to hear no more out of you." He removed the shirt and turned his back to her.

"Another picture," Sarah Ruth growled. "I might have known you was off after putting some more trash on yourself."

Parker's knees went hollow under him. He wheeled around and cried, "Look at it! Don't just say that! *Look* at it!"

"I done looked," she said.

"Don't you know who it is?" he cried in anguish.

"No, who is it?" Sarah Ruth said. "It ain't anybody I know."

"It's him," Parker said.

"Him who?"

"God!" Parker cried.

"God? God don't look like that!"

"What do you know how he looks?" Parker moaned. "You ain't seen him."

"He don't look," Sarah Ruth said. "He's a spirit. No man shall see his face."

"Aw listen," Parker groaned, "this is just a picture of him."

"Idolatry!" Sarah Ruth screamed. "Idolatry! Enflaming yourself with idols under every green tree! I can put up with lies and vanity but I don't want no idolator in this house!" and she grabbed up the broom and began to thrash him across the shoulders with it.

Parker was too stunned to resist. He sat there and let her beat him until she had nearly knocked him senseless and large welts had formed on the face of the tattooed Christ. Then he staggered up and made for the door.

She stamped the broom two or three times on the floor and went to the window and shook it out to get the taint of him off it. Still gripping it, she looked toward the pecan tree and her eyes hardened still more. There he was—who called himself Obadiah Elihue—leaning against the tree, crying like a baby.

WHEN HE'S AT HIS MOST BRAWLING

Patricia Goedicke

The woman in his belly stirs.
She nudges with her armfuls of blood
The hard walls of his abdomen.
Is it her black eelgrass hair
Terrifies him?
He makes a word to evacuate her
But she knows a lot of airmail
When she hears it.
The onion skins he flies out to the world,
Full of transparent hostility,
Are not for her.
He thinks he's got her number
But deep in his hunter's body,
Tangled like a harp in his guts
She snuggles in
Like fur.
When he flexes his muscles,
Shoots off his mouth
Or gun, can't he hear her shriek
Under his hobnailed heart?
When he's at his most brawling
She's at her most brutally gentle
And all over him like a silk tent
Her shimmering laughter
Like iridescent ice-crystals
Shatters the high notes
Of his dark hysteria.

A TREE, A ROCK, A CLOUD

Carson McCullers

It was raining that morning, and still very dark. When the boy reached the streetcar cafe he had almost finished his route and he went in for a cup of coffee. The place was an all-night cafe owned by a bitter and stingy man called Leo. After the raw, empty street, the cafe seemed friendly and bright: along the counter there were a couple of soldiers, three spinners from the cotton mill, and in a corner a man who sat hunched over with his nose and half his face down in a beer mug. The boy wore a helmet such as aviators wear. When he went into the cafe he unbuckled the chin strap and raised the right flap up over his pink little ear; often as he drank his coffee someone would speak to him in a friendly way. But this morning Leo did not look into his face and none of the men were talking. He paid and was leaving the cafe when a voice called out to him:

"Son! Hey Son!"

He turned back and the man in the corner was crooking his finger and nodding to him. He had brought his face out of the beer mug and he seemed suddenly very happy. The man was long and pale, with a big nose and faded orange hair.

"Hey Son!"

The boy went toward him. He was an undersized boy of about twelve, with one shoulder drawn higher than the other because of the weight of the paper sack. His face was shallow, freckled, and his eyes were round child eyes.

"Yeah Mister?"

The man laid one hand on the paper boy's shoulders, then grasped the boy's chin and turned his face slowly from one side to the other. The boy shrank back uneasily.

"Say! What's the big idea?"

The boy's voice was shrill; inside the cafe it was suddenly very quiet.

The man said slowly, "I love you."

All along the counter the men laughed. The boy, who had scowled and sidled away, did not know what to do. He looked over the counter at Leo, and Leo watched him with a weary, brittle jeer. The boy tried to laugh also. But the man was serious and sad.

"I did not mean to tease you, Son," he said. "Sit down and have a beer with me. There is something I have to explain."

Cautiously, out of the corner of his eye, the paper boy questioned the men along the counter to see what he should do. But they had gone back to their beer or their breakfast and did not notice him. Leo put a cup of coffee on the counter and a little jug of cream.

"He is a minor," Leo said.

The paper boy slid himself up onto the stool. The ear beneath the upturned flap of the helmet was very small and red. The man was nodding at him soberly.

"It is important," he said. Then he reached in his hip pocket and brought out something which he held up on the palm of his hand for the boy to see.

"Look very carefully," he said.

The boy stared, but there was nothing to look at very carefully. The man held in his big, grimy palm a photograph. It was the face of a woman, but blurred, so that only the hat and the dress she was wearing stood out clearly.

"See?" the man asked.

The boy nodded and the man placed another picture in his palm. The woman was standing on a beach in a bathing suit. The suit made her stomach very big, and that was the main thing you noticed.

"Got a good look?" He leaned over closer and finally asked: "You ever seen her before?"

The boy sat motionless, staring slantwise at the man. "Not so I know of."

"Very well." The man blew on the photographs and put them back into his pocket. "That was my wife."

"Dead?" the boy asked.

Slowly the man shook his head. He pursed his lips as though about to whistle and answered in a long-drawn way: "Nuuu—" he said. "I will explain."

The beer on the counter before the man was in a large brown mug. He did not pick it up to drink. Instead he bent down and, putting his face over the rim, he rested there for a moment. Then with both hands he tilted the mug and sipped.

"Some night you'll go to sleep with your big nose in a mug and drown," said Leo. "Prominent transient drowns in beer. That would be a cute death."

The paper boy tried to signal to Leo. While the man was not looking he screwed up his face and worked his mouth to question soundlessly: "Drunk?" But Leo only raised his eyebrows and turned away to put some pink strips of bacon on the grill. The man pushed the mug away from him, straightened himself, and folded his loose crooked hands on the counter. His face was sad as he looked at the paper boy. He did not blink, but from time to time the lids closed down with delicate gravity over his pale green eyes. It was nearing dawn and the boy shifted the weight of the paper sack.

"I am talking about love," the man said. "With me it is a science."

The boy half slid down from the stool. But the man raised his forefinger, and there was something about him that held the boy and would not let him go away.

"Twelve years ago I married the woman in the photograph. She was my wife for one year, nine months, three days, and two nights. I loved her. Yes. . . ." He tightened his blurred, rambling voice and said again: "I loved her. I thought also that she loved me. I was a railroad engineer. She had all home comforts and luxuries. It never crept into my brain that she was not satisfied. But do you know what happened?"

"Mgneeow!" said Leo.

The man did not take his eyes from the boy's face. "She left me. I came in one night and the house was empty and she was gone. She left me."

"With a fellow?" the boy asked.

Gently the man placed his palm down on the counter. "Why naturally, Son. A woman does not run off like that alone."

The cafe was quiet, the soft rain black and endless in the street outside. Leo pressed down the frying bacon with the prongs of his long fork. "So you have been chasing the floozie for eleven years. You frazzled old rascal!"

For the first time the man glanced at Leo. "Please don't be vulgar. Besides, I was not speaking to you." He turned back to the boy and said in a trusting and secretive undertone, "Let's not pay any attention to him. O.K.?"

The paper boy nodded doubtfully.

"It was like this," the man continued. "I am a person who feels many things. All my life one thing after another has impressed me. Moonlight. The leg of a pretty girl. One thing after another. But the point is that when I had enjoyed anything there was a peculiar sensation as though it was laying around loose in me. Nothing seemed to finish itself up or fit in with the other things. Women? I had my portion of them. The same. Afterwards laying around loose in me. I was a man who had never loved."

Very slowly he closed his eyelids, and the gesture was like a curtain drawn at the end of a scene in a play. When he spoke again his voice was excited and the words came fast—the lobes of his large, loose ears seemed to tremble.

"Then I met this woman. I was fifty-one years old and she always said she was thirty. I met her at a filling station and we were married within three days. And do you know what it was like? I just can't tell you. All I had ever felt was gathered together around this woman. Nothing lay around loose in me any more but was finished up by her."

The man stopped suddenly and stroked his long nose. His voice sank down to a steady and reproachful undertone: "I'm not explaining this right. What happened was this. There were these beautiful feelings and loose little pleasures inside me. And this woman was something like an assembly line for my soul. I run these little pieces of myself through her and I come out complete. Now do you follow me?"

"What was her name?" the boy asked.

"Oh," he said. "I called her Dodo. But that is immaterial."

"Did you try to make her come back?"

The man did not seem to hear. "Under the circumstances you can imagine how I felt when she left me."

Leo took the bacon from the grill and folded two strips of it between a bun. He had a gray face, with slitted eyes, and a pinched nose saddled by faint blue shadows. One of the mill workers signaled for more coffee and Leo poured it. He did not give refills on coffee free. The spinner ate breakfast there every morning, but the better Leo knew his customers the stingier he treated them. He nibbled his own bun as though he grudged it to himself.

"And you never got hold of her again?"

The boy did not know what to think of the man, and his child's face was uncertain with mingled curiosity and doubt. He was new on the paper route; it was still strange to him to be out in the town in the black, queer early morning.

"Yes," the man said. "I took a number of steps to get her back. I went around trying to locate her. I went to Tulsa where she had folks. And to Mobile. I went to every town where she had folks. And to Mobile. I went to every town she had ever mentioned to me, and I hunted down every man she had formerly been connected with. Tulsa, Atlanta, Chicago, Cheehaw, Memphis . . . For the better part of two years I chased around the country trying to lay hold of her."

"But the pair of them had vanished from the face of the earth!" said Leo.

"Don't listen to him," the man said confidentially. "And also just forget those two years. They are not important. What matters is that around the third year a curious thing begun to happen to me."

"What?" the boy asked.

The man leaned down and tilted his mug to take a sip of beer. But as he hovered over the mug his nostrils fluttered slightly; he sniffed the staleness of the beer and did not drink. "Love is a curious thing to begin with. At first I thought only of getting her back. It was a kind of mania. But then as time went on I tried to remember her. But do you know what happened?"

"No," the boy said.

"When I laid myself down on a bed and tried to think about her my mind became a blank. I couldn't see her. I would take out her pictures and look. No good. Nothing doing. A blank. Can you image it?"

"Say Mac!" Leo called down the counter, "Can you imagine this bozo's mind a blank!"

Slowly, as though fanning away flies, the man waved his hand. His green eyes were concentrated and fixed on the shallow little face of the paper boy.

"But a sudden piece of glass on a sidewalk. Or a nickel tune in a music box. A shadow on a wall at night. And I would remember. It might happen in a street and I would cry or bang my head against a lamppost. You follow me?"

"A piece of glass . . ." the boy said.

"Anything, I would walk around and I had no power of how and when to remember her. You think you can put up a kind of shield. But remembering don't come to a man face forward—it corners around sideways. I was at the mercy of everything I saw and heard. Suddenly instead of me combing the countryside to find her she begun to chase me around in my very soul. *She* chasing *me*, mind you! And in my soul."

The boy asked finally: "What part of the country were you in then?"

"Ooh," the man groaned, "I was a sick mortal. It was like smallpox. I confess, Son, that I boozed. I fornicated. I committed any sin that suddenly appealed to me. I am loath to confess it but I will do so. When I recall that period it is all curdled in my mind, it was so terrible."

The man leaned his head down and tapped his forehead on the counter. For a few seconds he stayed bowed over in this position, the back of his stringy neck covered with orange furze, his hands with their long warped fingers held palm to palm in an attitude of prayer. Then the man straightened himself; he was smiling and suddenly his face was bright and tremulous and old.

"It was in the fifth year that it happened," he said. "And with it I started my science."

Leo's mouth jerked with a pale, quick grin. "Well none of we boys are getting any younger," he said. Then with sudden anger he balled up a dishcloth he was holding and threw it down hard on the floor. "You draggle-tailed old Romeo!"

"What happened?" the boy asked.

The old man's voice was high and clear: "Peace," he answered.

"Huh?"

"It is hard to explain scientifically, Son," he said. "I guess the logical explanation is that she and I had fleed around from each other for so long that finally we just got tangled up together and lay down and quit. Peace. A queer and beautiful blankness. It was spring in Portland and the rain came every afternoon. All evening I just stayed there on my bed in the dark. And that is how the science come to me."

The windows in the streetcar were pale blue with light. The two soldiers paid for their beers and opened the door—one of the soldiers combed his hair and wiped off his muddy puttees before they went outside. The three mill workers bent silently over their breakfasts. Leo's clock was ticking on the wall.

"It is this. And listen carefully. I meditated on love and reasoned it out, I realized what is wrong with us. Men fall in love for the first time. And what do they fall in love with?"

The boy's soft mouth was partly open and he did not answer.

"A woman," the old mad said, "without science, with nothing to go by, they undertake the most dangerous and sacred experience in God's earth. They fall in love with a woman. Is that correct, Son?"

"Yeah," the boy said faintly.

"They start at the wrong end of love. They begin at the climax. Can you wonder it is so miserable? Do you know how men should love?"

The old man reached over and grasped the boy by the collar of his leather jacket. He gave him a gentle little shake and his green eyes gazed down unblinking and grave.

"Son, do you know how love should be begun?"

The boy sat small and listening and still. Slowly he shook his head. The old man leaned closer and whispered:

"A tree. A rock. A cloud."

It was still raining outside in the street: a mild, gray, endless rain. The mill whistle blew for the six o'clock shift and the three spinners paid and went away. There was no one in the cafe but Leo, the old man, and the little paper boy.

"The weather was like this in Portland," he said. "At the time my science was begun. I meditated and I started very cautious. I would pick up something from the street and take it home with me. I bought a goldfish and I concentrated on the goldfish and I loved it. I graduated from one thing to another. Day by day I was getting this technique. On the road from Portland to San Diego—"

"Aw shut up!" screamed Leo suddenly. "Shut up! Shut up!"

The old man still held the collar of the boy's jacket; he was trembling and his face was earnest and bright and wild. "For six years now I have gone around by myself and built up my science. And now I am a master. Son. I can love anything. No longer do I have to think about it even. I see a street full of people and a beautiful light comes in me. I watch a bird in the sky. Or I meet a traveler on the road. Everything, Son. And anybody. All stranger and all loved! Do you realize what a science like mine can mean?"

The boy held himself stiffly, his hands curled tight around the counter edge. Finally he asked: "Did you ever really find that lady?"

"What? What say, Son?"

"I mean," the boy asked timidly. "Have you fallen in love with a woman again?"

The old man loosened his grasp on the boy's collar. He turned away and for the first time his green eyes had a vague and scattered look. He lifted the mug from the counter, drank down the yellow beer. He head was shaking slowly from side to side. Then finally he answered: "No, son. You see that is the last step in my science. I go cautious. And I am not quite ready yet."

"Well!" said Leo. "Well well well!"

The old man stood in the open doorway. "Remember," he said. Framed there in the gray damp light of the early morning he looked shrunken and seedy and frail. But his smile was bright. "Remember I love you," he said with a last nod. And the door closed quietly behind him.

The boy did not speak for a long time. He pulled down the bangs on his forehead and slid his grimy little forefinger around the rim of his empty cup. Then without looking at Leo he finally asked:

"Was he drunk?"

"No," said Leo shortly.

The boy raised his clear voice higher. "Then was he a dope fiend?"

"No."

The boy looked up at Leo, and his flat little face was desperate, his voice urgent and shrill. "Was he crazy? Do you think he was a lunatic?" The paper boy's voice dropped suddenly with doubt. "Leo? Or not?"

But Leo would not answer him. Leo had run a night cafe for fourteen years, and he held himself to be a critic of craziness. There were the town characters and also the transients who roamed in from the night. He knew the manias of all of them. But he did not want to satisfy the questions of the waiting child. He tightened his pale face and was silent.

So the boy pulled down the right flap of his helmet and as he turned to leave he made the only comment that seemed safe to him, the only remark that could not be laughed down and despised:

"He sure has done a lot of traveling."

EPILOGUE

Is this how all women view men? Do men agree that these are the visions that should rule their lives? Do these women writers sufficiently understand the male reality—or have they overlooked or underemphasized something? Do they, for instance, overvalue relatedness and undervalue separateness? I do not know. But I deeply hope that this book will help foster healing dialogue among men and women on these and other questions so that we can create a society for our children and grandchildren that is less tortured by destructive gender socializations.

SELECTED BIBLIOGRAPHY

Bacon, Margaret Hope. *Mothers of Feminism: The Story of Quaker Women in America*. New York: Harper & Row, 1986.

Belenky, Mary Field, et al. *Women's Ways of Knowing*. New York: Basic Books, 1986.

Benstock, Shari, ed. *Feminist Issues and Literary Scholarship*. Bloomington: Indiana University Press, 1987.

Brod, Harry, ed. *The Making of Masculinities: The New Men's Studies*. Boston: Allen and Unwin, 1987.

Bronner, Edwin S. *William Penn's Holy Experiment: The Founding of Pennsylvania, 1681–1907*. New York: Temple University Publications, 1962.

Chodorow, Nancy. *The Reproduction of Mothering: Psychoanalysis and the Sociology of Gender*. Berkeley: University of California Press, 1978.

Christian, Barbara. *Black Women Novelists: The Development of a Tradition*. London: Greenwood Press, 1980.

Cornillon, Susan Koppleman. *Images of Women in Fiction: Feminist Perspectives*. Bowling Green, Ohio: Bowling Green University Popular Press, 1972.

Dinnerstein, Dorothy. *The Mermaid and the Minotaur: Sexual Arrangements and Human Malaise*. New York: Harper, 1977.

Donovan, Josephine, ed. *Feminist Literary Criticism: Explorations in Theory*. 2nd ed. Lexington: University Press of Kentucky, 1989.

———. *Feminist Theory: The Intellectual Traditions of American Feminism*. 2nd ed. New York: Frederick Ungar, 1992.

Doyle, James. *The Male Experience*. 2nd. ed. Dubuque, Iowa: William C. Brown, 1989.

Doyle, J., and Michele A. Paludi. *Sex and Gender*. 2nd ed. Madison, Wis.: Brown and Benchmark, 1989.

Eagleton, Mary, ed. *Feminist Literary Theory: A Reader*. Oxford: Blackwell, 1986.

Ehrenreich, Barbara. *The Hearts of Men: American Dreams and the Flight from Commitment*. New York: Anchor Press/Doubleday, 1983.

Eisler, Riane, and David Loye. *The Partnership Way: New Tools for Living and Learning, Healing Our Families, Our Communities and Our World*. San Francisco: Harper, 1990.

Fetterly, Judith. *The Resisting Reader: A Feminist Approach to American Fiction*. Bloomington: Indiana University Press, 1978.

Fryer, Judith. *The Faces of Eve: Women in the Nineteenth Century American Novel*. New York: Oxford University Press, 1976.

Gerzon, M. *A Choice of Heroes: The Changing Face of American Manhood*. Boston: Houghton Mifflin, 1982.

Gilbert, Sandra M., and Susan Grubar. *The Madwoman in the Attic: The Woman Writer and the Nineteenth Century Literary Imagination*. New Haven, Conn.: Yale University Press, 1979.

———. *No Man's Land: The Place of the Woman Writer in the Twentieth Century*. Vols. 1 & 2. New Haven, Conn.: Yale University Press, 1989.

Gilligan, Carol. *In a Different Voice: Psychological Theory and Women's Development*. Cambridge: Harvard University Press, 1982.

Gilmore, David. *Manhood in the Making: Cultural Concepts of Masculinity*. New Haven, Conn.: Yale University Press, 1990.

Greene, Gayle, and Coppelia Kahn, eds. *Making a Difference: Feminist Literary Criticism*. New York and London: Methuen, 1985.

Griffin, Susan. *Woman and Nature: The Roaring Inside Her*. New York: Harper and Row, 1979.

Keen, Sam. *Fire in the Belly: On Being a Man*. New York: Bantam Books, 1991.

Kimmel, Michael, ed. *Changing Men: New Directions in Research on Men and Masculinity*. Newbury Park, Calif.: Sage 1987.

Kimmel, Michael and Michael Messner, eds. *Men's Lives: Readings In The Sociology of Masculinity*. 2nd ed. New York: Macmillan, 1991.

Kolodny, Annette. "Dancing Through the Mindfield: Some Observations on the Theory, Practice, and Politics of a Feminist Literary Criticism." *Feminist Studies* 6 (1980): 1–25.

———. *The Lay of the Land: Metaphor as Experience and History in American Life and Letters*. Chapel Hill: University of North Carolina Press, 1975.

———. *The Land Before Her: Fantasy and Experience of the American Frontiers, 1630–1860*. Chapel Hill: University of North Carolina Press, 1984.

———. "Some Notes on Defining a Feminist Literary Criticism." *Critical Inquiry* 2 (1975): 75–92.

Komarovsky, M. *Dilemmas of Masculinity: A Study of College Youth*. New York: W.W. Norton, 1976.

Lewis, R.W.B. *The American Adam: Innocence, Tragedy, and Tradition in the Nineteenth Century*. Chicago: University of Chicago Press, 1955.

Maccoby, Eleanor E., and Carol N. Jacklin. *The Psychology of Sex Differences*. Stanford, Calif.: Stanford University Press, 1974.

McGill, Michael. *The McGill Report on Male Intimacy*. New York: Harper & Row, 1985.

Mills, Sara, et al. *Feminist Readings/Feminists Reading*. Charlottesville: University Press of Virginia, 1989.

Moers, Ellen. *Literary Women: The Great Writers*. New York: Oxford University Press, 1976.

Moi, Toril. *Sexual/Textual Politics: Feminist Literary Theory*. New York and London: Methuen, 1983.

Newman, Judith, and Deborah Rosenfelt, eds. *Feminist Criticism and Social Change: Sex, Class, and Race in Literature and Culture*. New York and London: Methuen, 1985.

Pagels, Elaine. *Adam, Eve and the Serpent*. New York: Random House, 1988.

Pleck, E.H., and J.H. Pleck. *The American Man*. Englewood Cliffs, N.J.: Prentice Hall, 1980.

Pleck, J.H. *The Myth of Masculinity*. Cambridge: MIT Press, 1981.

Pleck, J.H., and J. Sawyer. *Men and Masculinity*. Englewood Cliffs, N.J.: Prentice Hall, 1974.

Rubin, Lillian B. *Intimate Strangers: Men and Women Together*. San Bernardino, Calif.: Borgo Press, 1990.

Sedgwick, E. *Between Men: English Literature and Male Homosocial Desire*. New York: Columbia University Press, 1985.

Segal, Lynne. *Slow Motion: Changing Masculinities, Changing Men*. New Brunswick, N.J.: Rutgers University Press, 1990.

Seidler, Victor J. *Rediscovering Masculinity: Reason, Language, and Sexuality*. London and New York: Routledge, 1989.

Selden, Raman, and Peter Widdowson. *A Reader's Guide to Contemporary Literary Theory*. 3d ed. Lexington: University Press of Kentucky, 1993.

Showalter, Elaine, ed. *The New Feminist Criticism: Essays on Women, Literature, and Theory*. London: Virago, 1986.

———. *Speaking of Gender*. New York: Routledge, 1989.

Smith, Barbara. *Toward Black Feminist Criticism*. New York: Out and Out Books, 1977.

Spacks, Patricia Meyer. *The Female Imagination*. New York: Avon Books, 1976.

Tolles, Frederick B., and E. Gordon Alderfer, eds. *The Witness of William Penn*. New York: Macmillan, 1957.

Tong, Rosemarie. *Feminist Thought: A Comprehensive Introduction*. San Francisco: Westview Press, 1989.

Wallace, Terry S., ed. *A Sincere and Constant Love: An Introduction to the Work of Margaret Fell*. Richmond, Ind.: Friends United Press, 1992.

INDEX

About the Editor

PATRICIA ELLEN MARTIN DALY is Associate Professor of Communication Arts at Neumann College in Aston, PA. She is also a journalist, literary scholar, gender studies specialist, and editor, and is the author of *Introduction to Literature: Critical Thinking, Reading, and Writing* (1992), *Using Critical Thinking Skills* (1988), as well as twelve feminist fairy tales. Along with Peggy Pizzo, she is the coauthor of "Family Supports as a Public Policy Priority," a white paper she and Pizzo presented to the National Women's Economic Justice Center.

ISBN 0-313-29095-4

90000>

HARDCOVER BAR CODE